Disability Ethics and Preferential Justice

Disability Ethics

— AND —

Preferential Justice

A Catholic Perspective

M ARY J O I OZZIO

GEORGETOWN UNIVERSITY PRESS | WASHINGTON, DC

The publisher is not responsible for third-party websites or their content. URL links were active at time of publication.

Library of Congress Cataloging-in-Publication Data

Names: Iozzio, Mary Jo, author.
Title: Disability ethics and preferential justice : a Catholic perspective / Mary Jo Iozzio.
Description: Washington, DC : Georgetown University Press, 2023. | Includes bibliographical references and index.
Identifiers: LCCN 2022008186 (print) | LCCN 2022008187 (ebook) | ISBN 9781647123086 (hardcover) | ISBN 9781647123093 (paperback) | ISBN 9781647123109 (ebook)
Subjects: LCSH: Disabilities—Religious aspects—Catholic Church. | Disabilities—Moral and ethical aspects. | People with disabilities—Care—Moral and ethical aspects. | Social justice—Religious aspects—Catholic Church.
Classification: LCC BV4460 .I59 2023 (print) | LCC BV4460 (ebook) | DDC 259/.4—dc23/eng/20221004
LC record available at https://lccn.loc.gov/2022008186
LC ebook record available at https://lccn.loc.gov/2022008187

♾ This paper meets the requirements of ANSI/NISO Z39.48-1992 (Permanence of Paper).

24 23   9 8 7 6 5 4 3 2 First printing

Printed in the United States of America

Cover design by Erin Kirk
Cover image PSALM 85. Copyright 2003 by John August Swanson, Serigraph, 24" × 28.75", www.JohnAugustSwanson.com
Interior design by BookComp, Inc.

the person with disability is a privileged interlocutor of society and the church
Committee for the Jubilee Day of the Community
with Persons with Disabilities

In thanksgiving for the community of scholars with disability:
my interlocutors and friends of the AAR Standing Committee
on the Status of People with Disability in the Profession
and its Religion and Disability Studies Group.

— CONTENTS —

── FOREWORD ──

Disability Ethics and Preferential Justice: A Catholic Perspective by Mary Jo Iozzio, Catholic ethicist and senior scholar in disability studies, argues well the need for strong and clear Catholic approaches that address global and local ethical issues undergirding persons with disabilities. Attentive to personal and communal experiences and to empirical data concerning persons with disabilities by the World Health Organization, the United Nations, legal regulations through the Americans with Disabilities Act, and disability studies, Mary Jo makes a necessary and compelling case of accompaniment and advocacy for persons with disability, the world's largest minoritized and basically ignored group of persons totaling about 1.75 billion of the planet's 7.5 billion people. In the end, Mary Jo calls for a disability ethics that engages a preferential justice for persons with disabilities who are created in the image and likeness of God and are thereby integral relational members of the Body of Christ.

I have known Mary Jo for nearly twenty years from when I was a newly minted PhD/junior scholar to my current status as a tenured full professor. Most significantly, she has been instrumental in helping to facilitate my professional development/scholarship in Catholic theological ethics. Mary Jo invited me to speak at a conference that she sponsored; contribute a book chapter to her edited collection of essays; contribute to an international newsletter on Catholic ethics, *The FIRST*, for which she was editor of the North American Forum; and now to write the foreword to her book on disability ethics. Mary Jo has been a wonderful colleague. I am so grateful to know her and to appreciate who she is as a teacher, a scholar, and an advocate for all.

In matters of this text, Mary Jo recognizes that praise must be given to the Church for its teachings and to the consistency of its message on the sanctity of all human life as well as the dependence of all human life on God for the goods of creation and for God's continual intervention into all human affairs. However, she contends that a practical reality of exclusion remains true for persons with disability and other members of the Catholic communion (e.g., those belonging to gender, racial/ethnic, and language minorities) who have been and continue to be marginalized—if not by physical obstacles then by prejudice, discrimination, and ignorance—from the common weal. Furthermore, people with disability too often are excluded from access to many social goods readily enjoyed by the nondisabled, including church worship and participation in sacramental life, health care, education, nourishment, employment, sustainable environment, recreation, and friendship.

Still, Mary Jo believes that the Catholic Church has an unwavering stake in the care of persons and communities of people with disability as much as it has a stake in the care of the nondisabled. In this book, she seeks to concretize and actualize more powerfully the reality of the Church that subsists in Jesus Christ, the Crucified Disabled God. She seeks to concretize and actualize more powerfully the theological anthropology that all human beings are created in the image and likeness of God and are integral to the Body of Christ.

To speak directly to the specific moral concerns of marginalization, exclusion, and abuse related to people with disability, Mary Jo develops her ideas and understandings of a preferential justice for persons with disabilities through the employment of an ethics committed to Catholic social teaching decision-making methodology. This methodology encompasses the four resources of Christian ethics: *experience* in light of social analysis on disability, *reason* as it relates to the natural law and the common good in the context of disability, *revelation* as it concerns sacred scripture and tradition on disability, and *theological reflection in Church life* in light of disability. Chapters 1 through 4 strategically and logically expound on each of these aspects of the methodology. Chapter 5 offers some practical recommendations in the Church's commitments to accessibility and inclusion of persons with disability.

Furthermore, for Mary Jo this preferential justice for persons with disability originates not only from Catholic social teaching principles of human dignity, solidarity, and the promotion of peace but also from liberationist insights. Liberationist insights reveal that Jesus Christ always exemplified and embraced fully a preferential option for the poor, vulnerable, and marginalized in his earthly mission and ministry. As mentioned above, Mary Jo submits that people with disability have been and continue to be marginalized, despised, discriminated against, prejudged, and excluded from accessing the goods of society, experiences that have an adverse effect on the ability to realize the principles of human dignity, solidarity, and the promotion of peace. A liberationist worldview offers strong support to and for persons with disability, as it also illuminates a preferential justice for persons with disability.

Hence, as a way to better conceptualize and nuance a preferential option for the poor, vulnerable, and marginalized, Mary Jo champions the idea of a preferential justice for persons with disability. Her development of this preferential justice emerges from a theological anthropology that views persons with disability along with the nondisabled as integral relational members of the Body of Christ, created equally in the image and likeness of God.

I am so elated that Mary Jo has paid attention to personal and communal experiences, global data and perspectives, and other empirical evidence to support her championship of justice for persons with disability. I am thrilled that she employed the resources of her discipline—moral theology—to argue for a preferential justice for persons with disability. I believe deeply that Mary Jo's work makes important contributions to the global Church, disability studies, theological ethics, the academy overall, and society. Thank you, Mary Jo!

Shawnee M. Daniels-Sykes
Professor of Theology
Mount Mary University
Milwaukee, WI

— PREAMBLE —

Disability is a global reality about which too few register a thought of its prevalence. As a result, too few people without immediate experience or regular encounter with persons with disability remain unconcerned with this largest and most diverse minority of people across the globe (at least 15 percent of Earth's human population). Moreover, the likelihood of able-bodied/able-minded persons joining this minority increases with age if not by accident or by diagnosis of Alzheimer's disease, arthritis, depression, diabetes, heart disease, multiple sclerosis, Parkinson's disease, and other changes to health. No geographic location is immune from this prevalence, particularly in relation to the vicissitudes of contemporary life, though poverty increases and exacerbates vulnerability to being born with or acquiring a disability in one's lifetime. *Disability Ethics and Preferential Justice* is one response to a dearth of theo-ethical reflection on this critical concern for the requirements of justice in the vein of basic human functioning capabilities as the material of the common good, the means of which would be distributed with a preferential safeguard for persons and communities of people with disability.

Introduction

Disability Ethics and Preferential Justice: A Catholic Perspective unfolds with a general introduction to the work of disability studies scholars and their interlocutors. Throughout, I draw from materials developed by social scientists and their conversation partners in the humanities and health sciences as well as from the systematic, moral, and ecclesial disciplines in the Catholic theological tradition. Critical theory remains a prominent lens through which I examine much of this subject.[1] In the broadest sense of the term, critical theory in disability studies draws on exposing personal and structural or systemic forms of domination in which one group, in this case the able-bodied, exercises (knowingly or not) coercive and abusive normative power over another group, in this case people with disability. As such, disability studies considers the current state of affairs experienced by this or that person with disability or this or that community/groups of people living with similar conditions to expose disabling injustice, the deconstruction of assumptions regarding able-bodied/able-minded normativity in humankind and its impositions of hegemonic uniformity and enforced conformity to its norms, and the means of social and political action to support human flourishing with a preferential option for individuals and communities of people with disability.

I do not engage Judaism or Islam in this text. Nevertheless, as traditions that are parent and sibling to Christianity, much can be written about the contemporary interest in exploring how disability figures in their scriptures, reflections, and religious practices. Jewish and Muslim scholars engage disability studies in ways similar to this work. A minimalist sample here from these traditions acknowledges the like-minded trajectory of their efforts. For example,

> The Jewish Federation of North America supports a Committee on Inclusion and Disabilities with the same themes that secular and Christian organizations hold: accessibility, acceptance, accommodation, and welcome. Of course, the Christian tradition owes much of its ethical mandates to its Jewish elders and the law, prophets, and wisdom literature. "Social inclusion reflects values that are inherent to Jewish life: *Derech Eretz* (respectful behavior), *Chesed* (compassion), *K'vod Habriot* (encouraging dignity for all), and *Tikkun Olam* (repairing the world and making it a better place)."[2]
>
> Islam has initiatives that call for action in consciousness raising about, increasing access for, and inclusion of people with disability in the *Umma* (community), since, in the eyes of Allah, everyone is created equal in dignity and in honor. "In Islam, a person's worth is based not on any physical or material characteristics but on piety. Piety includes both faith in the tenets of Islam and a genuine attempt to adhere to Islam's obligations to the best of one's ability."[3] The Quran and hadith present disability as a morally neutral reality, neither a punishment from God nor a blessing; rather, all are encouraged to follow the practice of Prophet Muhammad, who extended hospitality and welcome to people with disability in his home, as companions, and with him in prayer.

Following this introduction, I present first a primer on disability basics. Second, I review the contributions made and data compiled by the United Nations and the World Health Organization regarding the prevalence of disability and the comorbid realities of poverty among the vast majority of people with disability in both developed and developing contexts. Third, I explore the traditions in Catholic theology of natural law with a focus on the common good as it applies to diversity in humankind inclusive of people with disability. Fourth, I present a

Trinitarian theological anthropology on the *imago Dei* (image of God)[4] with a view to the insights of Catholic social teaching. Fifth, I apply the liberation lens of Catholic social teaching with a preferential justice for those who are poor and otherwise marginalized, oppressed, or silenced on account of their disability. I conclude with reflections on the ethical imperatives of inclusion that bear on the dominant able-bodied/able-minded other toward the many diverse individuals and communities of people with disability in the Church and the world.

In addition to my own work in this text (like many seemingly able-bodied/able-minded persons, I have experienced temporary disability and have also attended to intimate physical, emotional, and social care of family members in need), I asked Catholic colleagues with similar disability intimacy and experience to contribute a thought or two on each chapter's subject. I am grateful for their generosity and contributions to this project. Their confidence and support are uniquely characteristic of colleagues in the guild of disability scholarship.

Shawnee M. Daniels-Sykes, RN, PhD, professor of theology and ethics at Mount Mary University (Milwaukee, Wisconsin) graciously accepted my invitation to write the foreword for the project from the vantage point of her teaching and research in ethics, medical/nursing care, and the generally unpredictable episodic experience of chronic health conditions. Miguel J. Romero, MDiv, ThM, ThD, assistant professor of religious and theological studies at Salve Regina University (Newport, Rhode Island), engages moral theology and Catholic social teaching with a view toward disability and mental illness (Miguel and I collaborated previously on an issue of the *Journal of Moral Theology*).[5] Jana Bennett, MDiv, PhD, professor of religious studies and department chair, University of Dayton (Dayton, Ohio), lectures and writes often on disability, technology, and religious thought through the lens of bioethics. Matthew Gaudet, PhD, lecturer of engineering ethics, Santa Clara University (Santa Clara, California), combines his engineering background with research interests in disability, education, peace, and social ethics. Lorraine Cuddeback-Gedeon, MDiv, PhD, director of mission and ministry at Mercy High School (Baltimore, Maryland), is passionate about social justice and works through an interdisciplinary lens alongside fieldwork that raises voices and experiences from the margins, especially of persons with intellectual and developmental disability. Maria Cataldo-Cunniff, MA, MTS, board certified chaplain (formerly at Boston's Children's Hospital and Phillips Academy, Andover, Massachusetts) and dear friend and editor, writes, lectures, and advocates for the empowerment that comes with disability justice. And retired colleague from Barry University (Miami Shores, Florida) Valerie Turner, DMin, my first personal editor in matters of work related to disability, has kept me honest, challenged my presumptions, and graced me with her friendship.

Personal Disclaimer

I began work in disability studies following the diagnosis of a severe genetic anomaly with the second pregnancy of a dear cousin. The diagnosis followed my introduction to the social construction model of disability in 1994 when reading "Toward a Feminist Theory of Disability" by philosopher Susan Wendell a year after my youngest brother died of AIDS.[6] My brother, Norman P. Iozzio, MD, was a laboratory pathologist. I mention him because my cousin had remarked to me that if Norman were alive he would know how to respond to the diagnosis determined by genetic testing and the prognosis presumed by the genetic counselors about the outcome of that pregnancy. Involved as I was in bioethics, she turned to me. She had been encouraged to abort the fetus since the anomaly of mismatched and incomplete genes was sure to express in a failure of the neonate to thrive.[7] Such bias is both sadly and alarmingly commonplace among prenatal genetic counseling and medical professionals alike.[8] Such a course of action was unthinkable to my cousin and her husband, an affront to their sensibilities about vulnerability and the precious nature of nascent life. Today her child is twenty-seven years old. It is to my cousin Deb's resilience and steadfast care of Bethany as well as to the many people I know who have disability, care for and love persons with disability, or both that I devote much of my research and writing on disability justice.

— 1 —

Disability Basics

When it comes to contemporary engagement with those phenomena typically organized under the heading "disability," there is a tendency among some ethicists to express uncritically problematic presumptions about the nature, meaning, and moral implications of disability. From the Catholic view, contemporary questions and challenges associated with disability are an extension of the gift of our asymmetrical creaturely nature, a manifestation of what is wondrous about our dignity, our grace-capacitated destiny, and a direct consequence of where we find ourselves—individually and collectively—amid the unfolding drama of the history of redemption. We are fragile beings whose creaturely freedom is forged in the dynamic intercourse of our limitations, our dependencies, and our innate vulnerability to impairment, illness, and injury. Theological attention to and reflection upon these intersections provide important insight for thinking well about disability today. Alternately, guided by narrowly functionalist anthropological principles and binary divisions of humanity into able/disabled can lead to ways of thinking that are irreconcilable with the Christian understanding of the human being.

Miguel J. Romero

In the TEDx presentation "It's Time to Talk about the World's Largest Minority," 2018 Michigan high school graduate Nina Farahanchi reveals a reality, discloses an interest, and admits a privilege that defies the experience of most of the world's people with disability. In less than thirteen minutes Farahanchi dispels many myths and stereotypes that nondisabled people hold about people with disability.[1] She offers the United Nations (UN) and World Health Organization (WHO) statistics that confirm the worldwide prevalence and largest minority status of people with disability. Farahanchi is blind and shares her story with rhetorical questions to the audience about "appearances" that challenge the dominant American narratives and attitudes about disability. A first-generation Iranian American, she knows well the negative and stereotypical assumptions about race, gender, and class that stigmatize and segregate many people in the United States. She identifies the intersections of identities that complicate encounters of visible or perceived difference. And she calls her audience to approach encounters with "other/different" others through a posture of respect, inclusivity, and empathy: as the largest and most diverse minority group of the globe, people with disability deserve no less.

I take Farahanchi's TEDx talk as an apt introduction to the phenomenon of the intersections and prevalence of disability worldwide, a perennial phenomenon only recently recognized as such. My concern, related to Farahanchi's, is disability justice. The ethical imperatives of justice for people with disability are obvious once the subject of and persons with disability are acknowledged as can be found, for example, in subsequent protections against discrimination in the United States that have been encoded within the Civil Rights Act of 1964 and the Voting Rights Act of 1965 and extended in the Americans with Disabilities Act of 1990 and subsequent amendments. The theological approaches are less known and perhaps even less adequately considered as having import for the secularized matters of the rule of law, the distribution of goods, and access to the multiple and multivalent arenas of human commerce from health care to education, employment, housing, worship, recreation, and a sustainable environment. The UN and the WHO have approached the subject of these imperatives under the rubrics of human rights, personal integrity, and the promotion of human flourishing with reference to the exercise of basic human functioning capabilities.

Today's classification of disability types follows generally the WHO's *International Classification of Functioning, Disability, and Health.*[2] The classification distinguishes between body functions, body structures, activities and participation, and environmental supports or lack thereof among individuals with disability. To use the language of more common parlance, the functions reflect what are ordinarily called "the purpose of" mental, sensory, voice, organ, metabolic, reproductive, neural-muscular-skeletal, and skin systems; the structures refer to a person's engagement of procedures or steps involved with voluntary and involuntary movement. Activities and participation consider the degree to which individuals engage both functions and structures, from cognitive, affective, and locomotive activity to self/family/community/ social/civic care. Environmental factors include attention to the presence or absence of support for an individual's participation in community, integral human development, and flourishing.

Thus, conditions of disability fall into one or multiple classifications of developmental, intellectual, mental, physical, and sensory functions. In a similar vein, many people have co-occurring symptomatic dysfunctions, disabilities, and health complications. Under the Americans with Disabilities Act, the categories that qualify a person for accommodations of individualized support or relief are expressed in physical or mental impairments that interfere with major life activities: affective disorders, autism, blindness, cognitive disability, deafness, emotional/developmental delay, hearing impairment, intellectual disability, muscular/physical/ skeletal impairment, neurological impairment, other health impairment, and specific learning disability.[3] These UN and WHO initiatives and Americans with Disabilities Act legal precedents cohere with a baseline understanding of human capability that takes the contexts and particularities in which individuals and communities live as key to unlocking everyone's basic human functioning capabilities.

As many of us in Western contexts have become accustomed to gender-inclusive and race-equity language, we have also become aware of the terms used in the past, and at times still heard today, that either exclude or insult outright persons and people with disability of all kinds and also insult, belittle, or ridicule the nondisabled (think of verbal and physical bullying) through negative associations regarding this or that disability.[4] Throughout this work I adopt a person-first vocabulary with an agenda of respectful inclusivity. I am aware that this adoption may suggest a paternalist slant, but that is not my intention. Where available, I defer to the voices of persons who have immediate experience with disability. Thus, as the United Spinal Association instructs, "People with disabilities are individuals with families, jobs, hobbies, likes and dis-likes, and problems and joys. While the disability is an integral part of who they are, it alone does not define them. Don't make them into disability heroes or victims. Treat them as individuals."[5] On a related note, I include offensive vocabulary terms retrieved from the ancient and more recent historical past only for instructive purposes regarding their use. In so doing, I adopt the methodology of critical theory that has been adapted to the social model of disability, a model that locates the disabling effects of capability functioning impairment as a result of the constructed failed accessibility experienced in environmental/physical, social/structural, and attitudinal/discriminatory barriers.[6]

Words Matter: Disability Terminology

The WHO recognizes that disability "is an umbrella term, covering impairments, activity limitations, and participation restrictions."[7] Among the terms that have become now standard nomenclature, the WHO dis-tinguishes three types of disability:

Impairment: A physical and/or sensory stumbling block in body
    function or structure.
Activity limitation: Impediment(s) to participation.
Participation restriction: A combination of physical, attitudinal,
    ideological, medical, and social barriers.

Rather than measure or define disability with the mistaken notion of a universal norm, the WHO adopts a biopsychosocial model. This model integrates the medical models that generally identify disability as a char-acteristic of a person with the social models (e.g., charity, environmental, minority, moral, and rights) that name the external conditions that are not inherent to the person with disability. These conditions make partic-ipation difficult if not impossible for the person with disability to access many of the goods and services readily available to the nondisabled.[8]

The models of disability offer a shorthand of characteristics that have worked for good and for ill in matters concerning persons with disability. While the biopsychosocial model distinguishes medical exigencies unique to an individual from the social environment the individual inhabits, by itself the model tends to focus on the biomedical condition as the first order of business. Helpful for medical needs, this model regards disability as an impairment that needs to be treated, cured, fixed, or rehabilitated.

The alternate to the medical model was developed by people with disability and is the approach I use most for my arguments in disability ethics and preferential justice. In the social model, disability is defined "as the disadvantage or restriction of activity caused by a contemporary social organization which takes little to no account of people who have physical impairments and thus excludes them from participation in the mainstream of social activities."[9] Further defining the construction of the social model of disability in its negatively discriminating application is the Social Role Valorization approach to understanding diverse human interaction that exposed the institutionalization of persons deemed "other," especially persons with disability.[10] Reasons given for institutionalization included deviance from the "main" with physical or functional impairment, race/ethnicity/gender, and all presumed dangerous thereby. Both developments advance a more expansive social model of disability that interrogates the environments wherein people conduct their lives with greater or less ease.

Throughout this work I use both group and individual references: people with disability and person(s) with disability. So as to avoid tendencies of overgeneralization, I use the singular "disability" (the plural is acceptable) unless the context indicates or requires otherwise.[11] Further, I use people-first language following the norm developed by persons with disability and their coadjutors at the National Center on Leadership for the Employment and Economic Advancement of People with Disabilities, "a collaborative of disability, workforce, and economic empowerment organizations."[12] Cautiously, I reference person(s) and people with disability as if homogenous—they are not: the diversity among and between individual persons with disability is equal to that among the nondisabled as well as between you (reader) and me (author) in our strengths and weaknesses except for the likelihood that very many people with disability live under conditions of extreme poverty and will therefore lack opportunities of upward social mobility. My generic use is deliberate for illustrative purposes even as it too fails to attend to the unique experiences of persons with this or that disability. For example, a person with physical disability who uses an assistive mobility device for locomotion will face physical obstacles in navigating from points A to B unless the terrain to be traversed is smooth and relatively level; a person with sensory disability (sight, sound, touch) will face obstacles in regard to information communicated through inaccessible means; and a person with cognitive or developmental disability will face obstacles to education, employment, or socialization where assumptions of worth (gained by these activities or undeveloped by lack thereof) likely hold sway.

As the WHO *World Report on Disability* advises, "Generalizations about 'disability' or 'people with disabilities' can mislead. Persons with disabilities have diverse personal factors with differences in gender, age, socioeconomic status, sexuality, ethnicity, or cultural heritage. Each has his or her personal preferences and responses to disability."[13] In writing and speaking, I follow the general rule of people first. Thus, if I know a person's name, I will refer to the person by name; alternately, I may refer to the person as someone/a person with cerebral palsy. As I argue throughout, disability is a common feature representing other expressions of the diversity—not an anomaly—present in humankind.

A Brief History of Experience

With exceptions, historically people with disability have not been treated well.[14] Their treatment has been identified and outlined for us by social science academics, psychology and nursing professionals, and humanities scholars in a system of models that distinguish one manner of treatment—with positive or negative effect—from another. Contemporary studies offer an approach to this history through the models of disability that are related closely to the ways in which the nondisabled and dominant codified their perceptions of people with disability according to the social roles that the nondisabled and dominant have assigned to them. The most common models of disability are religious-moral (sinner-saint), medical (intervention-prevention), and social (physical and attitudinal barriers and exclusion).[15] Parallel to these models are social roles, with the most recognizable to which individuals and communities of people with disability have been assigned being sick, subhuman, menace, pitiable, burden, holy innocent, inspirational, amusing, and blessing.[16] Regardless of model or role, each of these interpretations includes a greater or less degree of stigma: the defining mark of otherness that clears the way to marginalization and to greater or lesser degrees of direct oppression and violence.[17] The models offer a shorthand reference to understanding the presumptive attitudinal barriers that people with disability and their companions encounter all too frequently—to which Farahanchi alludes in her TEDx talk—to this day.

The theological underpinnings that support the movement to include people with disability in all arenas of human interaction present an imperative for theological reflection and for the Church so that all may enjoy the fullness of life. Those with the power to make and shape societies have been grossly mistaken in their judgment about the value and dignity belonging to people with disability and others who do not conform to hegemonic social norms. Those mistaken judgments are the basis of a history of maltreatment (not just mistreatment) that many people with disability have endured, a history that has been largely ignored and likely intentionally unrecorded for its blatant affront to human dignity as well as for the extreme cruelty of the perpetrators (similar to the gross abuse of African Americans held captive in slavery and by Jim Crow). In effect, people with disability themselves and their stories of success and failure and of loves and losses have been silenced over the course of time. However, that culture of silence is no longer acceptable: newborns, infants, children, and adults have been neglected, abused, and exterminated because of the presence of a disability in their lives.[18] Despite our unease with this brutality, their history is a critical part of the history of all humankind, a history that each of us must own if the mistakes and harms against them and others are not to be repeated, if reparations are to be made to those victimized, and if ideological and physical structures are to be rehabilitated, perpetrators are to be forgiven, and communities are to be reconciled.

In brief, though difficult to uncover,[19] the history of approaches to disability follows an overlapping series of categorizations. The categories begin with attempts by those with power and authority, however gained, to understand the presence of this or that disability and to interpret the value or disvalue of individuals with disability for the communities in which they were present. Among those first authorities were religious leaders and seers across the world's traditions. Those authorities were confirmed and at times challenged by the authority of scientists, doctors, and other cognoscenti. Confirming the social constructions of disability, those seated in the legal/sociopolitical/colonial realms of power institutionalized in law and custom the concept of and individuals with disability. Mostly as a result of the victors and those with power dominating narratives that tell the history they want recorded, this series of categorizations has been characterized by silence and the absence of the voices of people with disability themselves.[20] Fortunately and as a result of rising consciousness among the dominant, people with disability are now part of the retrieval and narration of the story inclusive of their experiences.[21]

With 15 percent to potentially 25 percent of people worldwide having one or more disabilities today (up to 1.75 billion of 7.6 billion people), it is reliably indisputable that persons with disability have been among the members of the human economy from antiquity to the present. Contemporary studies offer an approach to this history through the models of disability. These models are closely related to the ways that the nondisabled typified their perceptions of people with disability according to the social roles that the nondisabled and dominant have assigned to them. As noted above, the common models of disability are the religious-moral, the medical, and the social constructions. Additional precisions include approaches to or (false) understandings of persons with disability that reflect models of tragedy/charity, expert/professional, rehabilitation, economics, rights, and empowerment.[22] Parallel to the models are social roles, recognizable in the assignment of persons and communities of people with disability as sick or as nonhuman (as menace or angel) or commodified to suit another's purpose.[23] Again, regardless of model or role, these approaches are stigmatizing, marking an otherness that gives way to shame, oppression, and violence toward persons with disability.[24]

To the extent that those who have held power and authority record history, their resolutions concerning disability resulted in the marginalization of individuals and communities of people with disability on account of the causes those powers presumed were at fault for the conditions present. Among the causes these history makers attributed to disabling conditions are divine punishment for some sin (either one's own or one's parents), consorting with evil, an imbalance of humors, maternal stress during pregnancy, bestiality, menstruation, and astrology. Each of these causes encouraged perceptions that persons with disability were more animal or otherworldly than human, could tolerate environmental extremes and malnutrition, and were dangerous to the societies in which they lived. These conclusions gave license to harm persons with disability with impunity by "taming" them, sequestering them, or worse.

Scandalously, many individuals with disability—feared and loathed by the nondisabled—would have been exposed at or near birth or otherwise ostracized once the presence of a disability became known.[25] Infanticide by exposure was widespread, and in some state-sponsored cultic systems, the practice was mandatory. Some early Greek medical texts included information about recognizing defects at birth, in the first months, and in the early years so as to determine whether a child with disability is worth raising before resources are lost on caring for that child.[26] Aristotle too recommended laws to prevent the rearing of "deformed" children and to deny deaf children access to schools, since they would burden the progress of the nondisabled children of the community.[27] In Greco-Roman antiquity it would not have been uncommon for newborn girls and newborns with visible disability to be abandoned or left in a crude cradle at a crossroads or near a market, gymnasium, or temple with some possibility of being taken up (and likely enslaved) or tossed into a river by their patriarchs. Consider the following:

> After the birth of a child there is an anxious day or two for the poor young mother and the faithful nurses.—Will he [the father]

"nourish" it? Are there boys enough already? Is the disappointment over the birth of a daughter too keen? . . . Or does the child promise to be puny, sickly, or even deformed? If any of these arguments carry adverse weight, there is no appeal against the father's decision. He has until the fifth day after the birth to decide. In the interval, he can utter the fatal words, "Expose it!" [28]

Equally troubling and perhaps more horrifying, some children with disability were mutilated by parents—or overseers and other wardens, who depended on income from begging for their household maintenance—to increase the pity value others might assess on them and thereby increase almsgiving to their cause. [29] Less brutal but not less disturbing were practices that exhibited individuals with disability in courts of power as a sign of blessing, as entertainment, or to arouse pity and extend charity. Among other curiosities, the Roman gladiator games included the spectacle of fights between interchangeably short people, the deaf, other people with varying disability, women, and animals.

Judaism and Christianity fared a little better by prohibiting direct killing. However, some of the biblical texts reflect the perception that impairments signal something ungodly having been done (sin) or an evil spirit on the loose. [30] Consider the dialogue on theodicy in the book of Job. His interlocutors are quite certain that he or a member of his family surely sinned and brought this affliction on him and his children. [31] With this and other biblical texts, the religious model of disability takes hold and locates the presence of disability as punishment for some wrongdoing now in need of prayer, reparation, and expiation in order to be undone. Where the disability persists, the individual and the individual's family, tribe, or clan would ordinarily bear the stigma of disabling wrongdoing and its guilt-associated shame. Contemporary examples include the shame that many people harbor over the presence of mental illness in the family and, similarly though on the decline, the shame that surrounds many people living with HIV and AIDS and their families. The silencing that comes from being shamed is definitive.

The early medieval period made way for the custom of caring for the sick, those with disability, and the poor. Outside of the support of their natal homes, persons with disability were often reduced to poverty and resorted to begging as a principal means of income. Wanting to follow the example of Jesus, who attended to those who were marginalized for this or that stigma, Christians began to extend compassion to the less fortunate. By the height of the Middle Ages in Europe, a "period of organized beggary" led to guilds open to people with disability in which leaders emerged and rules and languages were developed by the guild members.[32] The guilds represent a welcome initiative by some of today's standards. Yet, this same period saw the institution of "idiot cages" that kept individuals with disability confined, while the cage protected those who consumed the spectacle beyond the bars. Where cages were insufficient or when the masses tired of this or that caged group, the "ship of fools" provided another form of distance to keep people with disability apart from the main by exploiting them as members of traveling carnival/horror/freak sideshows for port residents and visitors alike.[33]

And then came the development of institutions. Founded as a result of a system of hostels for pilgrims on their way to a holy site for both blessings and cures, hospitals for the sick and incurable became asylums for the insane and invalid. With the advent of the Enlightenment project to reject the old and quaint in favor of a rational order, new scientific ways of conceiving the individual in society and the common good of society brought to the fore utopian concerns of a more perfect communion, overtly including an underlying concern for the dangers lurking in any near presence of people with disability. The isolation of institutions provided "safety" for the nondisabled community and gave rise to better or worse care for those institutionalized; institutions also (inadvertently?) delivered a captive population to study objectively. With concentrated access to people with a diverse array of disabilities, doctors and scientists began to investigate the causes of various disabilities using newly advanced medical and empirical methodologies. Some of this early science fueled the eugenics movements of the nineteenth and early to mid-twentieth centuries through the subsequent sterilization of people with disability and other suspicious folk.[34] Consider the scientific "proofs" of a biological basis for the categories of race and the subsequent discrimination against nonwhite peoples, especially peoples of African descent in the United States, that labeled many deviant and resulted in institutionalization of a medical or penal sort. People from Mediterranean countries and Asia were also considered to be of "questionable genetic stock" and likely to either increase the number of feebleminded in the general population or the number of criminals who would become costly wards of the state; it would be better to prevent them from reproducing altogether.[35] As long as people were institutionalized and thereby isolated from general human commerce, they were—and those who remain institutionalized are—vulnerable to abuse, medical/experimental exploitation, and other dehumanizing injustices.

The confluence of social progress, science, and rational self-interest led to the systematic individualization and medicalization of all persons—those deemed "normal" and those deemed "othered"—as subjects (the normalized) and as objects (the aberrant/abnormal/disabled) of observation and study. This systematic program led to an ideology of disdain for, unease with, and distrust of any who did not conform to the putatively normative/ideal modern man. By the twentieth century, eugenic initiatives were set in Europe and the United States with sterilization programs and final solutions in a murderous holocaust of untold, unnumbered, and unaccounted hundreds of thousands of persons on account of their disability or creed. Scandalously still, eugenics and euthanasia by a different name continue apace with neonates, children, adolescents, and adults in their prime and elderly with disability as today's principal populations vulnerable to medical-social-scientific control.[36] While eugenics may not be institutionalized, it holds ideological power and is practiced widely in reproductive medicine and the selective abortion of fetuses. Similarly, euthanasia remains a threat in the form of withholding life support from a person—neonate, infant, child, or adult—who could thrive if given the chance, not heroic or extraordinary intervention but rather ordinary care.

This history belies the Christian tradition's recognition that every human being is created in the image and likeness of God; as such, no person is ever to be treated as an object to be discarded or to be experimented upon without consent, particularly at a time when diversity is increasingly being recognized as the calling card of God's creation and our inheritance.[37]

Norm Making, Norm Imposing, and Norm Challenging

In the world of dualistic segregations, superficially identifiable differences have been used to categorize and, invariably, establish hierarchies that ranked individuals and communities on the basis of their conformity to a norm. In the case of human norms, the dualisms of male/ female, spirit/body, white/nonwhite, heterosexual/homosexual, and nondisabled/disabled have designated de facto the second part of each pair as a defective version of the first part, which subsequently led to the oppression or patronization of the second by the first. However, when diversity, inclusive of people with disability, is presumed as normative, these dualisms lose their power to elevate one expression of diversity, however narrow or large, over the diversity of other expressions. When diversity is normative, dualisms no longer make sense: difference remains intact while the hierarchies collapse.

Elizabeth Johnson, building on the thinking of Paul Ricouer, considers how the symbol of God functions; for my purposes, I look to how that symbol rejects dualisms and points to a theological anthropology of radical dependence. "There is no subordination, no before or after, no first, second, and third, no dominant and marginalized. . . . The trinitarian symbol intimates a community of equals. . . . It models the ideal . . . of relational bonding that enables the growth of persons as genuine subjects of history in and through the matrix of community, and the flourishing of community in and through the praxis of its members."[38] In the world of mutual relationality, diversity in humankind— itself kaleidoscopic in form and fecund asymmetry even in disability—is the norm.

Once the dualisms artificially segregating one community from another are disempowered, two needs emerge: one that attends to the needs of those formerly ignored or oppressed and one that attends to diversity for the long haul, inclusive of adjustments and access to places previously denied to individuals and communities of people with disability and others discriminated against on account of their difference from "the putative norm." Rather than locating anthropological norms in superficially observable characteristics, an approach to human anthropological diversity locates the norms of humankind in the obligating features[39] and functional capabilities[40] belonging to every person by virtue of everyone's individual personhood. These "norms" are particularly suitable for human flourishing through relationality, which at an existential level is a condition that requires diversity.[41] A move beyond static anthropological norms to a dynamic facility in dependent relationship opens the dialogue on what constitutes being human wide enough to include diversity in humankind even to those previously deemed marginal, outliers, outsiders, and outcasts at best: persons with disability.

Along with the presumption of norms, since the Enlightenment the Western world has been preoccupied with liberal notions of autonomy and rational agency. Consider that Denis Diderot (1713–84), David Hume (1711–76), Immanuel Kant (1724–1804), Søren Kierkegaard (1813–55), Adam Smith (1723–90), and others constructed the validity of their arguments by moving from premises concerning human nature, *as they understood it to be* (and epitomized by the Anglo-European male), to conclusions concerning the authority of established moral rules and precepts.[42] These men inherited the privilege to argue the validity of and indirectly enforce their conceptions of norms that, to the chagrin of those who trespassed against them, persist today in functioning against many through hegemonic control. While I do not deny the contributions that these men have made to the cause of personal agency, denial of their narrow focus of "who really matters" requires interrogation with a hermeneutic of suspicion. Nevertheless, all must reckon with these notions that have influenced heavily the determinations of norms or lack thereof for human flourishing.

One of the norms championed in this thought pattern concerns the constellation of attributes of independence, self-determination, and individualism that presumably define the developmental maturity, if not the very humanity, of a person *as a human being*. This norm of developmental maturity pervades the political and medical-technological debates on the value of human life in its nascent or otherwise vulnerable (e.g., due to disability) state. This debate was dramatized in the 1972 play *Whose Life Is It Anyway?*[43] And this debate is rehearsed in trauma centers and obstetric offices throughout the country today: "I would be better off dead," "No one would want to live like that," "It would be better if you terminate the pregnancy now." When the hegemonic norms of independence are held as sacrosanct, it is no wonder that many would begin to think that any condition resembling dependence ought to be shunned or that death (or abortion for the fetus diagnosed with genetic anomaly) ought to be preferred. However, this thinking belies the experience of many persons with disability and betrays an injustice toward people with other stigmatizing semblances of need.[44] That is, many persons with disability report that they are happy and that except for the stigma associated with disabilities, their lives are satisfying.[45]

Sadly, much thinking among the nondisabled lacks any investigation on their part about life with disabilities, about mental or sensory acuity or physical changes that attend to aging processes, or about being the parent or sibling of a child with disability. Nevertheless, because most people will acquire a disability that leads to differing degrees of dependence at some point in their lives, thinking that death is preferable to life presents frightening prospects for anyone who becomes vulnerable due to age, accident, or disease. The prospect of active euthanasia following this line of thinking threatens everyone. In the spirit of independence and rugged individualism, too few recognize that life is precious and all too short for most regardless of disability. Further, every embryo that is allowed to develop into a fetus and be born is statistically miraculous: excluding contraception use, potentially procreative intercourse/periods of human fertility last between twelve and forty-eight hours monthly. Most heterosexual intercourse is therefore nonprocreative, and every life is indeed precious.[46]

Stigma

The historically predominant form of injustice imposed upon persons with disability is stigma. Stigma does not stand alone. A comprehensive definition of stigma recognizes a co-occurrence of its component parts, which constitute a permutation that depends on "othering," the primary assignment of certain people as outliers, outsiders, and outcasts. Such assignment includes labeling that rises as a result of a deviation from (hegemonic) norms; stereotyping that associates difference with negative assumptions (e.g., people with mental illness are generally dangerous); segregating "us" from "them," the nondisabled and normal from people with disability, by classifying negatively labeled persons as fundamentally different because they are fundamentally flawed (taken to the extreme, they are not really human); and diminished status and discrimination as a result of the three former components. Add these permutations to the power that is integral to stigma and the result is unjust discrimination and status loss that is widely manifest and embedded in social systems where people endure the power inequities that raise some over most. Moreover, "through the deployment of disabling and abling binary discourses alone or in combination, [biblical] texts create categories of stigmatized persons whom they seek to marginalize, as well as their antitype: categories of privileged persons who lack negatively constructed, stigmatized characteristics and possess valued traits."[47]

The assignment of stigma and associated labels to disabling conditions and to persons with disability appear in a variety of historical records with sometimes dreadful effect.[48] For example, the earliest use of the word "stigma" in English (1596) refers to circumcision as a kind of branding and a sign of subjection, by extrapolation, of Jewish men to God. By 1863 the term referred to the whipping marks inflicted upon slaves, subject to their owners, in the United States and the British colonies. Perhaps with this later meaning and as part of the cult of anti-Black racism in the United States especially, to be stigmatized would demand nearly absolute censure and condemnation. From ancient texts, physical and developmental conditions were judged as being auspicious or ominous, perverse and evil, or, more generously, another fact of mortal life.[49]

Just as Michel Foucault has provided a critical analysis of power and its abuses, stigma can figure in his "dividing practices" that objectify whole classes of people as "other." Foucault's analysis of power and its abuse expose the objectification of subjects, which reduces people to things (and thus quite disposable). With the imposition of these dividing practices, the subject is or soon becomes internally divided (think of internalized oppression or cognitive dissonance) and is just as surely soon divided from others. "This process objectifies [the subject]. Examples are the mad and the sane, the sick and the healthy, the criminals and the 'good boys.' These practices effectively legitimize segregation and social exclusion that categorize, classify, distribute and manipulate [the] subjects under [someone else's] control."[50] Once a class is so defined, it is easy to legitimize all manner of oppression, marginalization, and abuse, since, having been objectified/dehumanized, they no longer qualify for the protections afforded to the dominant or acceptable main. Not recognizably people, they are vulnerable to gross inhumanity.[51] Moreover, once stigma is assigned, the power of unjust discrimination becomes institutionalized: discrimination will be direct, the bias will be structurally and socially assumed, and both oppressor (in the form of superiority) and victim (in the form of inferiority) will internalize the hegemonic normativity of sexism, heterosexism, racism, ageism, and ableism.

Disabled

Again, in order to continue the reversal of the trajectory that history reveals, scholars in religion and disability have looked to formative texts in our traditions; for Christians, those texts include the Scriptures and theological reflection over the centuries that seek to uncover the meanings of God's being and acting in the world. Thus, the texts must be parsed in ways that uncover both literal and metaphorical meanings at the time of their composition and now in their postmodern reception. The words "disabled" and "disability" will not be found in the ancient or classical texts. Where, then, is evidence of disabling conditions and persons and communities with disability to be found? First, evidence can be retrieved by attending to words such as "blemished," "defective," "fool," "lame," and "possessed," among others found widely in Scripture[52] as well as in the classics and other literature.[53] For example, a search of these terms in the Bible yields the following number of occurrences with reference to human beings: blemished, 17; defective, 2; fool(ish), 225; lame, 27; and possessed, 9. Some of these references are metaphorically pejorative; that is, "calling out" blindness or deafness may refer to a person's ignorance of a matter of law or custom.[54] To retrieve similarly elusive labels in the work of Aristotle and Thomas Aquinas, searches for words such as "mad," "blind," and "lame" produce greater numbers—in the hundreds—of occurrence and are used to distinguish relief from certain domestic responsibilities and blame or to prevent persons with these conditions from entering into contractual and vocational activities where they may be vulnerable to abuse. Second, evidence is fairly certain in the proscriptions regarding classes of people with disability and their presence or participation in both ceremonial and common life.[55] "Persons with 'defects' are frequently stigmatized by biblical [and Qumran] authors, who also assign them marginal social positions."[56] Those positions result in prohibitions regarding cultic acts or exclusion outright.

Regardless of their use to protect the nondisabled from the "other" with disability, because labels objectify subjects, depending on the label attached to persons and the causes associated with their conditions, nondisabled people would favor or reject individuals objectified by tolerable or loathsome labels.[57] Thus, to the extent that persons with disability could entertain, they could be tolerated; to the extent that a disabling condition caused visceral recoil by the nondisabled or seemed threatening, those persons with disability would be removed from the company of the nondisabled. Moreover, depending on the permutation of co-occurring labels (e.g., women, foreign, hirsute, nonbinary plus disability), persons with disability would suffer greater or less severity of oppression.

Thankfully, another way of thinking about individuals and communities of people with disability and about the diversity of disability as variation in functioning capabilities has been raised by scholars with disability and their collaborators.

As noted, disability is present in the human community in fantastic diversity. Every person is unique in each one's own way as a distinguishing condition of diversity in the human community. Conditioned in this way, diversity does not eliminate anyone from belonging to the human communion. Further, as some disabilities accompany fetal development, others are acquired at the time of delivery, and still others develop over time or are acquired as a result of aging, injury, violence, accident, adverse or allergic reaction, or disease. And along the way, communion persists.

* * *

In the chapters that follow, I continue to unpack the complex yet commonplace understandings that disability holds in the imaginations of many who are not immediately affected by disability of one sort or another, that is, people with no personal experience themselves or among those with whom they have a personal relationship among persons with physical, developmental, intellectual, sensory, social, or behavioral disability. These understandings help or hurt the cause of justice at the heart of my interest in how theology can inform both abstract theorizing about disability and concrete responses to the needs of individuals and communities of people with disability, their families, and their allies. Further, given that poverty often accompanies conditions of disability, the traditions that concern the common good through the mechanism of the distribution of resources need to be figured in both theory and practice as an imperative response to the *imago Dei* that each of us bears to all and to one another.

— 2 —

Contributions from the
United Nations and the
World Health Organization

The UN and the WHO have been extolled as organizations that stand for greater accessibility and rights for people with disabilities. Yet I'm aware, as a deaf person, that it is one thing to discuss accessibility but quite another to become a disability-friendly society. As long as society continues to see disability only as a negative aspect of being human, we cannot truly cultivate a world where all people are treated as being made in God's image.

Jana Bennett

The United Nations (UN) explicitly recognizes human rights for persons with disability, and with the Convention of the Rights of Persons with Disabilities (2006) and its signatories, the UN has raised protections against discrimination, exploitation, and abuse of people with disability to the level of international law. The World Health Organization (WHO) works collaboratively with its partners across the globe in gathering data and local analyses of efforts to minimize the occurrences of acquired disability and to maximize the availability of adaptive and rehabilitation programs for people with disability. These organizations, global in nature and purpose, have benefited from the insights raised by people with disability and scholars working at the intersections of disability, religion, and justice.[1] The efficacy and opportunities of international coalitions available with these organizations remain, I submit, underutilized locally and globally. In what follows I challenge the ethics of simple accommodations to which many nations submit with a robust agenda of social justice that affirms and advocates for and with people with disability using the UN/WHO initiatives to inform a new paradigm for our churches and our world for the common good of all.

As noted in the introduction, taken as a whole population category, the UN and the WHO confirm that people with disability constitute the largest minority community of Earth's human population—almost 15 percent, or 1 billion of 7.6 billion people.[2] Closer to home, nearly 18 percent (59 million of the 320 million estimated) of noninstitutionalized people in the United States have documented disability (there may be as many as 4 million who remain institutionalized in the United States),[3] with many more undocumented (e.g., Medicare enrollees).[4] Globally, most people with disability live at or below local poverty levels. The tradition of the common good, which the UN affirms implicitly in its founding charter, offers incentive to respond materially to the basic needs that all people have of food, housing, education, health care, and employment. The biblical revelation of the *imago Dei*, while not referenced explicitly in these UN documents, serves as the basis of its Universal Declaration of Human Rights (UDHR) wherein the inherent dignity and equality of human beings is safeguarded by what I suggest are calls to reverence one another in ways countercultural to a consumerism that privileges some as it impoverishes most. And, I add to these international commitments that, with preferential justice, people with disability—especially for those among them who are poor—are to be reverenced equally as the *imago Dei* despite their disability or their poverty. This preferential justice can reorient common good and communal priorities so as to have their good served first.

The United Nations

The UN was established in 1945 "to practice tolerance, unite in peace for security, and promote the economic and social advancement of all peoples."[5] Since then, the UN has grown in power and influence over member states and the global community of concerned agents of change for both a secure present and a sustainable future. The organization has offices across the globe to support local development initiatives that essentially guide implementation of the 1948 UDHR and by which nations can measure their achievements in and protections of fundamental human rights in their communities.[6] Since 1971, the UN has given explicit attention to the concerns of people with disability leading up to declarations regarding the protection of rights owing to them: the International Year of Disabled Persons (1981); the adoption of a World Programme of Action concerning Disabled Persons (1982), inaugurating the commitment of a Decade of Disabled Persons (1983–92);[7] and, capping these UN initiatives, the Convention on the Rights of Persons with Disabilities (CRPD) of 2006.[8] The CRPD leads global international efforts in "reaffirming the universality, indivisibility, interdependence and interrelatedness of all human rights and fundamental freedoms and the need for persons with disabilities to be guaranteed their full enjoyment without discrimination."[9]

Along with other UN initiatives, the UN Department of Economic and Social Affairs (UNDESA) serves as a clearinghouse of international efforts to advance development and promote human rights, following the UDHR, for persons with disability. Three principal mandates inform the work of the Secretariat for the Convention on the Rights of Persons with Disabilities: the articles of the CRPD, the "Standard Rules on the Equalization of Opportunities for Persons with Disabilities," and the World Programme of Action concerning Disabled Persons.[10] These mandates together outline the commitments of government signatories to act with and for people with disability and to assist in international and national policy making and cooperation in regard to programs with and for people with disability. In the United States, the Centers for Disease Control and Prevention along with international bodies that operate offices in the United States maintains the Washington Group on Disability Statistics, which develops measurement tools and standardized questionnaires to record incidences of disability across the spectrum of physical, congenital, emotional, cognitive, and sensory conditions and the degrees of difficulty experienced by people with disability in reference to activities of daily living associated with the identified disabilities.[11]

In addition to these monitoring initiatives, the UNDESA identifies priority issues that include tools and resources to facilitate protections of the rights of people with disability,[12] as stated in the CRPD, Article 1: "to promote, protect, and ensure the full and equal enjoyment of all human rights and fundamental freedoms by all persons with disabilities, and to promote respect for their inherent dignity." In addition, there are web pages dedicated to disability initiatives under the UNDESA. The UNDESA identifies four focus areas, each of them attached directly or indirectly to the 2015 Millennium Development Goals (MDGs)[13] and the 2030 Sustainable Development Goals (SDGs):[14] "Women and Girls with Disabilities," "Monitoring of Disability-Inclusive Development," "Disability, Accessibility and Sustainable Urban Development," and "International Day of Persons with Disabilities—December 3."[15] Among the issues identified by the UNDESA—from accessibility to mainstreaming disability, disability and women, disability and HIV/AIDS, employment, health, and disasters and emergency situations—I focus here on the UN flagship report on disability and development, *Realization of the Sustainable Development Goals by, for, and with Persons with Disabilities*.[16]

In spite of President Barack Obama signing the CRPD in 2009, the United States has not ratified the treaty. This failure remains a curiosity for many more a decade later. Unfortunately, without ratification US participation globally in implementation, development, and collaboration in is hampered. Perhaps unsurprisingly, the US Congress could not reach consensus across the political divides in the predominantly two-party governance on this and other matters concerning global partnerships and the liberties belonging to trenchant individualism (e.g., parental rights), supposed conflicts with domestic law, and US sovereignty.[17] Sadly, in addition to a one-term president's public mocking of persons with disability (and others), subsequent attempts to revive the question in either Congress or the Senate Foreign Relations Committee have been met with the rancor of partisan politics, some concerning the unfounded claims above and others attributable to a failure to bring the treaty again to Congress. Perhaps with President Joe Biden and a Democratic majority in both congressional houses, ratification will be done.

The *Realization of the Sustainable Development Goals* report presents a "UN system-wide effort to examine disability" to determine how well people with disability have fared since the implementation of the SDGs (and post-MDGs of 2000–2015). The MDGs committed global leaders to reducing poverty worldwide by the year 2015 through a series of eight interrelated initiatives: eradicate extreme poverty and hunger; achieve universal primary education; promote gender equality and empower women; reduce child mortality; improve maternal health; combat HIV/ AIDS, malaria, and other diseases; ensure environmental sustainability; and form a global partnership for development. In December 2003 the UN General Assembly adopted a resolution to implement the World Programme of Action concerning Disabled Persons as part of the efforts contained within these MDGs.[18] That resolution was followed in subsequent assemblies, reports, and a "high-level meeting of the General Assembly on disability and development" that challenged the pace of integration and action to remedy the distance between UN concern for people with disability and the MDGs. A 2013 issue paper revealed the less than hoped for state of the integration of disability throughout the initiatives of the MDGs.[19]

The SDGs present "an urgent call for action by all countries . . . in a global partnership" for peace and prosperity for people and for the planet with eleven specific references to people with disability.[20] Like the MDGs, the seventeen SDGs are designed for action, from ending poverty to ensuring the future of our common home, all its inhabitants and ecosystems, and of the universe of which our solar system is a part. While the MDGs, principal focus was on eradicating poverty (MDG 1: Eradicate Extreme Poverty and Hunger) and the SDGs continue the emphasis on ending poverty, the links among the seventeen SDG goals make explicit the need to address development with an integrated approach inclusive of benchmarks that indicate success and measures of accountability among all partners and stakeholders. The SDGs commit global leaders and stakeholders to reverse the course of future peril if we fail to act now, through its seventeen interrelated initiatives:

1. End poverty;
2. end hunger;
3. ensure healthy lives;
4. ensure inclusive and equitable quality education;
5. achieve gender equality;
6. ensure clean water and sanitation for all;
7. ensure affordable and clean energy for all;
8. promote inclusive and decent work for all;
9. build inclusive, resilient, innovative infrastructure;
10. reduce global inequality;
11. make cities inclusive, safe, and resilient;
12. ensure responsible consumption and production;
13. take urgent action to reverse climate change;
14. conserve life underwater;
15. protect, restore, and promote terrestrial ecosystems;
16. promote peaceful inclusive societies and accountable institutions; and
17. strengthen global partnerships.

The *Realization* report finds that "despite the progress made in recent years, persons with disabilities continue to face numerous barriers to their full inclusion and participation" as well as "disproportionate levels of poverty; . . . lack of access to education, health services and employment; underrepresentation in decision-making . . . ; [and] discrimination and stigma on the grounds of disability."[21]

Internationally, people with disability remain among the least advantaged of all the world's people. As noted above and comprising at least 15 percent of the world's population, people with disability disproportionately rank among the world's most impoverished.[22] This likelihood of poverty is alarming: people with disability may make up 20 percent of the world's poorest citizens, and among those who are poorest, 80 percent of them are people with disability.

One household in every four contains a disabled member.... [And] 90% of all disabled children in developing countries still do not attend school and the literacy rate for disabled adults may be as low as 1%. One out of every three street children are children with a disability. Unemployment rates for persons with disabilities in many countries routinely reach two-thirds or more of all those with disabilities.

    ... As with many other marginalized populations, there are a variety of approaches—both disability inclusive and disability specific—that seek to incorporate persons with disabilities and disability issues into broader development work.... For example, where broad women's empowerment programmes do not reach women in an ethnic community, specific outreach programmes are often initiated. Reaching subgroups within the larger disabled population—for example, targeted HIV and reproductive health outreach programmes in sign language for deaf adolescents— should be no different.

    ... In this, disability should be regarded as a cross-cutting issue comparable to gender. No programme should be initiated without consideration for how persons with disabilities will be served, just as consistent and comprehensive attention as to how women will be affected and included is not expected for all programmes.[23]

In addition to the challenges exacerbating poverty levels among the world's people with disability, wars and armed conflict are responsible for a fair share of the incidences of preventable disabilities. Present-day ongoing conflicts in Afghanistan, Syria, Yemen, Somalia, Iraq, and Haiti, for example, present dreadful examples where millions of people have died and millions more are injured with the lasting impact of disability on their lives and the lives of their families and communities. Moreover, conflicts of this perpetual sort increase the vulnerability of people with disability by preventing their access to the basic needs for capabilities functioning while also increasing the ranks of people in need through disability acquired as a result of compromises to a community's infra- structure (e.g., roads and safe houses) and services (emergency and rou- tine medical care) as well as direct harm from the weapons machinery of war.[24] Human Rights Watch identifies combatants and civilians alike with war-related disability as the "invisible victims" of conflict,[25] and Handicap International reports on the multigenerational effects of these crisis-disabling casualties.[26] Much more can be said about this and other violent warring conflicts throughout the world.

At the 2018 Global Disability Summit, the World Bank Group—in collaboration with the United Kingdom, the International Disability Alliance, the government of Kenya, and the UN—committed its resources and influence to accelerate global action for disability-inclusive development and to "ensure the rights, freedoms, dignity and inclusion for all persons with disabilities."[27] Founded in 1944, the World Bank Group is the globe's largest development institution. With its mission to end extreme poverty and promote shared prosperity, the group funded the landmark *World Report on Disability* to recognize the prevalence of disability worldwide and support international efforts to reduce the poverty of people with disability and the incidence of disability. As such, the World Bank builds on the *World Report on Disability* and the SDGs 4 (inclusive education) and 9 (universal design) as well as initiatives specific to women and girls with disability and to people with disability in contexts of humanitarian crisis.[28] In particular, "the main objective of the 2018 *Disability Inclusion and Accountability Framework* is to support the mainstreaming of disability in World Bank activities. . . . The primary audience is Bank staff but it is also relevant to the Bank's client countries, development partners, and persons with disabilities."[29]

The World Health Organization

On a course that was parallel to the establishment of the UN and the World Bank Group, a series of meetings initiated by public health professionals from Western Europe, Asia, and the United States[30] led the then League of Nations (established after World War I) to recognize that "the equitable provision of health and welfare could reduce internal social conflicts and help prevent war."[31] Those meetings resulted in the League of Nations Health Organization in 1923. With the 1945 establishment of the UN and its mandated responsibilities for health and other matters of international cooperative concern, the League of Nations Health Organization was transferred to the UN under the newly designated World Health Organization to become the vehicle directing, coordinating, and monitoring global health.

The primary role of the WHO is to direct international health initiatives and lead partners in global health responses. The WHO enjoys this authorization by virtue of Article 25 of the UDHR, which states the right to "well-being . . . including food, clothing, housing and medical care [and] to security in the event of unemployment, sickness, disability, widowhood, old age or other lack of livelihood." With this right to well-being, the Constitution of the World Health Organization was adopted in 1946 by the International Health Conference "to promote and protect the health of all peoples" with the single objective of "the attainment by all people [throughout the globe] of the highest possible level of health."[32] It would be another twenty years—1966—before the UN International Covenant on Economic, Social, and Cultural Rights codified "the right of everyone to the enjoyment of the highest attainable standard of physical and mental health."[33] Although caution is in order on the potential conflation of health-to-illness as ability-to-disability, the WHO utilizes both the Human Rights model and the CRPD to recognize the barriers to well-being experienced by many people with disability and the failures to provide access to not only health care but also education, employment, family, community, and public life (goods that the World Bank Group has committed to making accessible to people with disability).

The WHO began to address disability through a lens more conducive to the social constructions of disability than the UN's earlier efforts in a series of publications: the *International Classification of Functioning, Disability and Health* (2001) and the companion classification *International Classification of Functioning, Disability and Health: Children & Youth Version* (2007); in collaboration with the World Bank Group, the first *World Report on Disability* (2011); and a *Global Disability Action Plan 2014–2021: Better Health for All People with Disability* (2015).[34] Unlike strictly medical models of disability, these documents reject simple determinations of interventions for this or that disability affecting this or that individual. Rather, and following the insights of social economist Amartya Sen, the WHO adopted a schema for determining the support or repression of human rights owing to all people on the basis of the expressions and degree to which they can exercise their "functioning capabilities."[35]

The WHO utilizes the UDHR model to address the global conditions affecting public and personal health broadly. Among the measures of health, the WHO accepts in principle the mid-twentieth-century critiques and a hermeneutics of suspicion that have been developing in the humanities and social sciences; these critiques are known as the social constructions of understanding phenomena of many kinds (e.g., race, sex, and gender), including the social constructions of disability introduced in chapter 1: disability basics/disability terminology.[36] These critiques gain argumentative force when they are examined through the lens of basic human functioning capabilities, developed by Sen with philosopher Martha Nussbaum, to measure the attainment of health.[37]

The WHO's *International Classification of Functioning, Disability and Health* and its companion *International Classification of Functioning, Disability and Health: Children & Youth Version* are the now standard operating metric regarding human well-being for all persons, not only persons with disability. Combined with the insights of the social constructions of disability, the WHO standards point directly to the variable local and context-specific conditions on the ground that contribute to a life of flourishing or a life of impoverished opportunity for all people, not just for those with disability. The WHO's comprehensive lens of functioning capabilities suggests the diversity of disability alongside the diversity of humankind: by way of affirming the wide expressions of humankind, the anthropological diversity of people with disability is, I argue, uniquely indicative of human beingness.[38]

Although the WHO does not venture explicitly into theological vocabularies, its recognition of diversity inclusive of people with disability exposes what is most true of human beings qua *imago Dei*: in order to be and to thrive, human beings must accept and affirm their relational dependence upon one another; in this anthropology, relationality is the sine qua non of diversity. Relational dependence, which I have identified elsewhere as radical dependence, is human unity in diversity; as such, dependence of the kind required for the support of human lives holds liberative normative force for all humankind, inclusive of people with disability.[39]

As a dynamic force, this norm of relational dependence requires nothing less than the affirmation of every person regardless of her/zir/his race, gender, or ability, and to the extent that many people with disability have been denied, the explicit, intentional, and robust affirmation of people with disability of any kind is long overdue.[40] Practically, the affirmation of dependence will require explicit, intentional, and robust access to the exercise and subsequent development of each person's functioning capabilities inclusive of a natural life span; physical health and opportunities for sexual satisfaction and reproductive choice; access to pain relief; use of creative, intellectual, and spiritual potential; relationships with others; self-determination; economic, social, and political participation and reciprocity; and ecological balance; recreation; noninterference; and freedom (the list of capabilities reads comprehensively and fluently like the 2030 Sustainable Development Goals). As Nussbaum instructs, basic human functional capabilities include

- being able to live to the end of a human life of normal length (not dying prematurely);
- being able to have good health (to have adequate nourishment and shelter, having opportunities for sexual satisfaction and choice in matters of reproduction, being able to move from place to place);
- being able to avoid unnecessary and nonbeneficial pain and to have pleasurable experiences;
- being able to use the senses (to imagine, to think, and to reason and to do these things aided by adequate education and to enjoy and produce aesthetic and religious materials);
- being able to have attachments to things and persons outside ourselves (to love those who love and care for us, to grieve at their absence, to experience longing and gratitude);

- being able to form a conception of the good and to engage in critical reflection about the planning of one's own life (to seek employment outside of one's home and to participate in political life);
- being able to live for and with others, to recognize and show concern for other human beings, and to engage in various forms of social interaction (being able to imagine the situation of another and have compassion for that situation, to have the capability for both justice and friendship, protection of freedom of assembly, and freedom of speech);
- being able to live with concern for and in relation to animals, plants, and the world of nature;
- being able to laugh, to play, and to enjoy recreational activities;
- being able to live one's own life and nobody else's (having certain guarantees of noninterference with certain choices that are especially personal and definitive of selfhood such as choices regarding marriage, childbearing, sexual expression, speech, and employment); and
- being able to live one's own life in one's own surroundings and context (this requires freedom of association and freedom from unwarranted search and seizure, a certain sort of guarantee of the integrity of personal property).[41]

As noted above and in association with the World Bank, the WHO published the first *World Report on Disability* in 2011. The *World Report* notes the nearly unimaginable diversity of gender, age, socioeconomic status, sexuality, ethnicity, and cultural heritage among people with disability[42] and recognizes further that "the disability experience resulting from the interaction of health conditions, personal factors, and environmental factors varies greatly."[43] Disability studies literature, led by scholars with disability and their allies, confirms that the experience of disability is multifarious and the experience of disadvantage is multidimensional, unnecessarily co-occurring not as morbidities but instead as a remediable fact of life for many. As people with disability defy the expectations of homogeneity and challenge by their survival the social constructions assumed in the unexamined inherited development and subsequent imposition of norms and standards—those hegemonic norms and standards have purposely or inadvertently "othered" and stigmatized them. Among the consequences of stigma is a de rigueur denial of access to the goods that contribute to well-being and human flourishing: personal-familial-social relationships, development and exercise of basic human functioning capabilities, and access to health care, education, employment, social services, and recreation.

One of the quantifiable metrics for measuring the likelihood of access to the goods that contribute to well-being is economic stability. Sadly and as a result of their lack of access to these goods, people with disability rank among the poorest members of most populations (a UK study reports a 47.4% poverty rate for people with disabilities!).[44] With the capabilities approach applied specifically to households that include a person or persons with disability, poverty is determined not singularly by material wealth or goods but instead by a standard of living conducive to functioning at capacity. Certainly, the basic goods of housing, education, health care, employment, and recreation number among these standards; however, a more accurate accounting of the wealth-to-poverty scale will be determined more thoroughly by how well these basic goods are accessed and enjoyed rather than by the quantity purchased and consumed.[45] Access to and enjoyment of goods by people with disability requires a holistic approach to the measurement of economic stability by, for example, a survey of the participants in any given venue: to the extent that the number of people with disability present reaches 15–18 percent of attendees/participants, access parity is met; where the numbers fail, access to the means of flourishing are difficult at best or denied outright, and poverty is likely found.

In sum, people with disability are more likely to be impoverished as a result of the social constructions of their being "other" and thereby are deemed as being unworthy of the common goods to which the nondisabled have frequent, ready, and unimpeded access.

A New Paradigm beyond Accommodation to Affirmation and Advocacy

This work is dedicated to moving beyond accommodation to affirmation and advocacy for people with disability, a people both marginalized and denigrated with impunity across time and place. In order to so move, a paradigm larger than accommodation is necessary. I do not mean to suggest that accommodations are no longer necessary. On the contrary, the dominant systems and structures of power have been none too generous when requests for accommodations to relieve the exclusion of people with disability from human commerce are made. It is not difficult to imagine responses to accommodations requests: "You want us to level the entry stairs to the Gothic facade of the church? A ramp will destroy the integrity of the architecture! Yes, it's better that you go elsewhere for worship or you can enter the building through the back door or the basement" (as if the person is unworthy of the main entrance; not only is the denial exclusionary, it is discriminatory and an affront to human dignity not unlike Jim Crow laws in the United States).[46] Other examples concern accommodation failures to protect children (and adults) with cognitive or developmental disability; many among them experience verbal, psychological, and physical abuse from rape to beatings to neglect. In 2017, the US Department of Education opened an investigation of the Philadelphia, Pennsylvania, school district into a complaint of systematic failure of the district to address "pervasive and severe bullying of students with disabilities . . . [where] the environment and opportunity for bullying and harassment" goes unchecked and where requests by parents to transfer their children to another school were declined.[47] The first example, of denied access, seems to be an isolated case. However, the experience of unwelcoming entryways is surprisingly common (moreover, where entryways remain inaccessible, the church or other institution is consciously or not indicating "No Service" for people with disability). The second example, regretfully also common, demonstrates the frequency of violence perpetrated upon children with disability (adults with disability are no less vulnerable).[48]

With the insights of the US civil rights movement and the work on behalf of justice among, with, and for African Americans, Indigenous peoples, people with disability, their caregivers, and their advocates have claimed their places within their communities and beyond to undo the outlier status assigned to them. Some of the rights to participate in all manner of personal, familial, educational, social, political, commercial, legal, and ecclesial activities that have been summarily denied to people with disability in the past are now recognized as belonging to them though they are enjoyed only sporadically. Sporadic access is dependent largely on awareness, particularly by those who hold the literal and figurative keys, of the desire among people with disability to so participate; this access depends on the will of the dominant power and authority to admit that there are obstacles blocking the participation of people with disability as much as they block—with stairs and with stares and sleights and shame—their way.

This clearly unacceptable state of affairs is no longer tolerable. The prevalence of disability throughout time and place needs today a reckoning with justice. Discrimination against people with disability—as with discrimination against nonwhite people of color as well as gay, lesbian, bisexual, transgender, intersex, and queer people and people belonging to nondominant religious or cultural traditions—must be named as yet another failure of the social constructions of norms defined in a world dominated by a strong and powerful few.

Since 2000, 206 communities have signed agreements with the US Department of Justice under its Project Civic Access to ensure that their citizens with disability enjoy the same services, programs, and activities that all others enjoy.[49] These agreements oblige communities to follow the Uniform Federal Accessibility Guidelines to meet architectural, procedural, and communication standards. Moreover, no qualified person with a disability may be excluded from participating in or denied the benefits of the programs, services, and activities by state and local governments and other public and private enterprises on account of a disability.

These measures have raised awareness of the presence of people with disability in the United States and beyond and, as noted in the introduction, have raised consciousness of the often scandalous ways that people with disability have been treated from the past to the present. Many of the reasons for this scandal rest in the social construction of disability, a model for understanding this history and its persistence from today's recognition of the power of norms to divide people into an "us" and a "them."[50] Such division is as much an attitudinal position as it is an obligatory stance among members of the dominant group toward the nondominant group as (unwelcome) "others."[51] In addition to othering/excluding/bullying, some reasons for scandal betray a failure to admit human interdependence on the multiple degrees and varying levels of relationships each human being requires to become, to develop, and to flourish until the end of our days.

✳ ✳ ✳

The law is certain: discrimination in matters of employment, programs, and services on the basis of disability is no longer tolerable. Fair enough. People with disability and their advocates ask now about access so as to enjoy the benefits of such guarantees; many others ask who will bear the cost. These questions provoke adherents of libertarianism and the Western myth of rugged individualism as it raises their suspicions about government interference in a free market and in the exercise of personal autonomy to disperse or withhold, for example, my wealth, my resources, and my claims to this or that as I deem right and so will. In chapter 3 I look at how the traditions of natural law and the common good inform disability-inclusive initiatives in accommodations, affirmations, and advocacy for and with people with disability.

— 3 —

Natural Law and the Common Good

I understand natural law as the communication of Divine Wisdom through God's authorship in creation itself. Since God created every particle in the universe to be as it is, there is wisdom to be gleaned from observing the natural structures of that creation. Taking natural law seriously, then, requires us to recognize that imperfections and impairments are a feature of creation, not a bug. We are all imperfect and impaired and that is by design. Our individual impairments render us vulnerable and our collective vulnerabilities draw us into the community that God intends for us to be.

Matthew Gaudet

Natural law has a long history in the traditions of thinking ethically about what human beings are to do and, I would add, how human beings are to be. I hold natural law not as a particularly prescriptive set of "laws" to be followed under penalty of sin but instead as a general presentation of the order of things living and inanimate (e.g., birds fly and fish swim "naturally," and in the twenty-first century, that human beings fly or swim is also quite "natural" but not really except for the human ingenuity to harness energy). To the extent that such an order is fairly observable, the traditions of natural law are readily confirmed in human practice in the arenas of human commerce about the good that human beings are to do, seek, and become, with their ends or purposes fixed in or on that which leads to human flourishing.

I take the common good to be part of the tradition of a teleological approach to natural law with the means of flourishing as its shorthand. From a teleological framework, I include the goods found in the development and exercise of the basic human functioning capabilities to be an expression of "the goods that all beings seek,"[1] the first dictum in excursus about natural law. As such, these goods are the ends that all human beings are thereby to have access to and enjoy. These common goods, as iterated in the principles and precepts of natural law, include self-preservation (food, shelter, health), procreation and child-rearing (generational family relationships), knowledge about what is true and right in our experiences (with and about God, creation, and our place in the scheme of things), and communal life (responsibilities each has to, with, and for others near and far). These goods point also to the teachings of the Catholic Church's tradition of the common good, those things necessary for both individual and community flourishing by means of the sufficient working order of societies—familial, educational, legal, political, social, religious, commercial, national, and global orders—in which all persons have a stake.[2] Moreover, access to these goods is fundamentally necessary to human flourishing, because without access many languish. Insofar as the basic human functioning capabilities cohere with the principles of natural law, access to the common good—what I suggest are those opportunities to develop and exercise one's capabilities so as to attain and enjoy the goods that all beings seek—pertains to all people, inclusive of people with disability for whom these opportunities have been all too often denied.

That anything should pertain to all people confirms the fundamental premises regarding our creation and the equal dignity with which each human being is endowed and to which Genesis 1:27, the US Declaration of Independence, the UN Charter, the Universal Declaration of Human Rights, and many Church documents attest.[3] As such, all human beings have a virtual obligation to develop the abilities—inherent to each albeit in variable and disproportionate measure across the capability spectrum—that lead, if given the opportunity, to flourishing and a good human life as a positive natural right and the province of human initiative.[4] Of course, these documents have weaknesses in their application, and as history proves, some people have been regarded "more equal" (in the sense of George Orwell's *Animal Farm*) than others by virtue of their sex, gender, race, class, religion, culture, and (perceived) ability.[5]

Nevertheless, if all human beings are equal, then the common goods outlined in natural law must be accessible by all and their distribution available in the degree needed to exercise their capabilities to be, to love, to learn, to engage, and to thrive. The common good functions here as shorthand for, as the Church teaches in Pope St. John XXIII's *Mater et Magistra*, "the sum total of those conditions of social living, whereby [people] are enabled more fully and readily to achieve their own perfection."[6] While it may be obvious that people with disability belong to the community of humankind, many have not been recognized as persons for whom access to the means of flourishing or the use of common goods are granted; they have been treated basely instead (cf. Deut. 32:5). Following the disposal and exposure in antiquity up to the medieval beggars, among the more scandalizing forms of "treatment" for people with disability in the fairly recent period of modernity, which continues to this day, are asylums and "convalescent" homes. Although many institutions for children and adults with disability have been shuttered, from the rise of sanatoriums to the prison-like settings of asylums,[7] obvious denials of the means to develop and exercise basic human functioning capabilities were commonplace for people with physical or developmental disability or both.[8] These failures to recognize the capabilities of persons with disability—from the development of capabilities to care for and love oneself to bodily integrity, communication, friendship, play, and literacy, in short, moral agency—were/are the equivalent to withholding the means to actualize natural law in access to the good(s) all human beings seek. At minimum, denials of voluntary social relationships exposed in often brutal institutional settings signal obstinacy on the part of the dominant power to acknowledge diversity in humankind as both revelatory and marvelous. Maximally, this failure denies the *imago Dei* and insults—dare I say blasphemes against[9]—God.

Moreover, when access to the goods that all people seek is denied on the basis of disability or other discriminating devices, their flourishing is compromised if not threatened *tout court*. Such a state of affairs belies the *imago Dei* in which each of us has been created and loved by God. Are we not all called to love likewise? In what follows I look to how the common good serves as the linchpin to understanding natural law as each of us seek goods necessary to both survive and thrive.

Natural Law

The purpose of exploring the role of natural law in matters related to people with disability arises directly from the quality of being human and acceptance of qualitative diversity present in people considered "outside of the main" by the representatives controlling the narratives of hegemonic normativity, that is, the normative diversity of nonwhite people of color; gay, lesbian, bisexual, transgender, intersex, and queer people; people belonging to nondominant religious or cultural traditions; and people with disability. Specifically, many people without disability have assumed that life with disability is a contradiction in the terms for what is good and right for human beings, that it may be better for people with disability to have not been born, and that such a life must be riddled with pain, tragedy, and, in general, despair. Such assumptions belie the experience of many people with disability.

As tradition has it, natural law is a fairly readily accessible means for abstracting a way of being in the world by giving attention to the basic functioning capabilities present across the experience of humankind in place of hegemonic norms that exclude many persons (often women and people with disability) putatively considered beyond the main. Contra hegemony, Thomas Aquinas instructs: to the extent that a law is a precept of reason directed to a common good by "someone"—God or the local magistrate—who has the authority to so do, natural law is the moral agent's "natural inclination to [reason's] proper act and [proper] end . . . whereby we discern what is good and what is evil" so as to "proceed to the more particular determinations of certain matters."[10] Aquinas's approach to natural law rests ultimately in his metaphysics of morals and his firm belief that all human beings have access to natural law through reason's apprehension of being/essence, that is, the individual's means of participation in eternal law.

The key to natural law is holding its parts in the right order. As Aquinas notes, the principle and precepts of natural law operate in distinct spheres within the economy of moral agency. As he has presented the metaphysics of the human act by distinctions between the movements of the human will *quantum ad exercitium* (as a primary act of the freedom to move or to be moved by the stirring of the faculty of reason to discover opportunities) and *quantum ad specificationem* (as a second act to intend and choose what the faculty of reason discerns is best),[11] the principle and precepts of natural law come to the fore as primary and secondary datum about the good and the right for human beings to have (or to be) and to do.

Thus, an application of natural law follows an apprehension by the practical reason (which is directed toward action) of the good. "Since every agent acts for an end under the aspect of [its being] good[,] . . . *the first principle* . . . is one founded on the notion of the good, viz., that good is that which all things seek after." From this apprehension, *the first precept* of natural law emerges hence: that "good is to be done and pursued, and evil is to be avoided. . . . [W]hatever the practical reason naturally apprehends as [a human] good (or evil) belongs to the precepts of the natural law as something to be done or avoided."[12] The secondary precepts of natural law concern the specification of goods that pertain to self-preservation, procreation and child-rearing; knowledge and the truth about God; and the ability to live and participate in society. Fundamentally, "it is proper to [human beings] to be inclined to act according to reason."[13]

Insofar as people with disability enjoy the basic functioning capabilities, these precepts are as knowable to them as they are to the nondisabled in our midst. These precepts and capabilities are the matrix for a contemporary understanding of the common good. Table 3.1 lists the "good" as outlined in natural law alongside the basic functioning capabilities for human flourishing.

The Common Good

In the tradition of Aristotle and his interlocutor Aquinas, justice of the virtue and governmental kind rather than prosecutorial—concerns what each of us owes to another not necessarily as a matter of the exchange of

TABLE 3.1.   Alignment of natural law and basic human functioning capabilities

Natural Law	Basic Human Functioning Capabilities
All beings seek the good; therefore, do good and avoid evil	The right to exercise one's capabilities without the injustices of discrimination
Self-preservation	A natural life span, physical health and well-being, self-determination, and noninterference
Procreation and child-rearing	Sexual satisfaction and reproductive choice
To know God and truth	Use of creative, intellectual, and spiritual potentials
To live in society, participate in social capital, and contribute to the common good	Relationships with others, economic-social-political participation and reciprocity, ecological balance, and recreation

goods and services but instead as a matter of the well-ordered structures that support the communities and societies of which each of us is a part. Aquinas is again instructive: "Now each his [one's] own is that which is due to [her/zir/]him according to equality of proportion. Therefore the proper act of justice is nothing else than to render to each one [her/zir/] his own."[14] Justice is the virtue that is considerate of the needs proper to persons as persons and that pertain to contractual agreements, the common good and resource distributions, and individual human flourishing.[15] The virtue of justice locates right action squarely on the mean of right relations, on justice itself. That is, for the tradition, the mean or measure of justice is justice; its defect is, simply, injustice. Therefore, when the virtue of justice is engaged, the just act is the giving to others their due according to commutative/contractual agreements, the distribution of resources, or retributive penalties pertaining to the common good.

Further, "justice by its name implies equality, it denotes essentially relation to another, for a thing is equal, not to itself, but to another."[16] The measure of distributive justice—what I take here as the common good—is thus the specification of the distribution of common goods according to a geometric proportion—a relation—between things and persons.[17] Such a proportion is rarely reckoned an equal amount; rather, geometry holds measurements based not on similarity but instead on suitable relations between things. A geometric proportion between persons and things would be based on individual and common needs in reference to the goods that contribute to human flourishing. Thus, the geometric proportion to be determined in a twenty-first-century first world context must identify the parties concerned (one person and another, one person and the community, a class of persons and the state) and the goods to be distributed (access to education, employment, health, and ecclesial, political, and social gatherings). These poles (two persons/entities and this or that good) provide the data for the determination of proportionality, and where the geometric equality of proportionate need among them emerges, there the common good is distributed and there justice will be rendered.

In the context of disability, justice is rendered as an accommodation for persons with disability, and such accommodations depend on access. In particular, justice is the geometric proportion between goods—access, accommodations, services, and the like—and persons, providing for the needs that some people with disability will have from time to time and those needs that are constant (accommodations of this sort are routinely provided to the nondisabled without much notice). Insofar as the Americans with Disabilities Act requires "reasonable accommodations" for persons with disability,[18] the law is clear—though stingy—about needs and the distribution of goods to meet, that is, to accommodate those needs. Building a disability-inclusive community, however, reveals that justice requires accommodations beyond the letter of the law to include an appreciation of the benefits that accommodations make for all people, not just those with disability, and to support those persons with disability who, for lack of this or that accommodation, could not express their potential as persons or personnel in an earlier period of time. Accommodations for persons with disability bring the equality of all persons with disability in line with calculations for the nondisabled regarding the three-way geometric proportion that renders justice in the distribution

of goods as meeting the interdependent needs of both individual flourishing and the common good flourishing of all.

Wherefore Justice?

Those of us who live in the United States now know that the Declaration
of Independence was written by and for white free able-minded men of
the colonies, an unarguably noninclusive position to hold today. Women
and Black folks would wait 144 years and 189 years, respectively, for
enfranchisement and the rights and freedoms protected by the US
Constitution, subsequent amendments, and the laws found in the Federal Code of Regulations. Many assume that these laws have leveled the
field sufficiently for social progress among women and people of color.
However, barriers reinforced by the social constructions of sex, gender, and race as well as institutionalized disadvantages against progress
among them prevents their development and advancement in the contemporary human economy.

Where many fail to recognize the persistence of disadvantages for
women and people of color, they also fail to recognize the profoundly
disadvantaged access to the conditions that support the development
and skills belonging to persons with disability: their basic human functioning capabilities to be, to learn and become proficient, and to thrive.[19]
Each of these groups has been denied an exercise of their autonomy.
Moreover, this failure relates to a certain (white and privileged) American hubris that imagines each and every one of us having the where-
withal and support required for success in life—each of us presumably
possessing a hegemonic Lockean "state of nature"[20]—if only we would
each just try harder, pull ourselves up by our bootstraps, and get to
work. What is not recognized by the dominant group is both their own
privilege and their denial of access to the common good of the many not
included in their class (e.g., women, people of color, and persons with
disability). That denial results in a compromised state of well-being as
well as reduced opportunities to contribute to the common good.

I understand the desire and need to protect (a libertarian) autonomy.
However, given the historical realities that people with disability as a

class have experienced, they have been denied development of their capacities—unique to individuals of every class—to maximize the exercise of their autonomy. Like women and people of color, people with disability are disadvantaged on account of institutionalized systemic injustices that denied (and continue to deny) them access to the means of acquiring the skills that would hone their potentials. To address this denial properly requires a return to the question of justice for and with people with disability. Reluctant though many will be to admit it, "individuals in [this US] libertarian state—however free and self-reliant they may appear—are nonetheless dependent on social conditions that are meant to account for many of their incapacities."[21] Those conditions include housing, education, health care, reliable protections from harm, and social infrastructure, all part and parcel of the common good, which supports the development of those basic human functional capabilities whereby human beings thrive despite the presence of this or that disability. That dependence must then be reckoned with whose responsibility it is to bear and to what extent the provision of common goods and services beyond the reach of most if not all members of the human community are met. Who, then, will bear this cost but a "civilized" society, and to what extent will this cost be calculated and distributed based on the proportionate geometric need that individuals will have from less to more on account of their transient and/or permanent disability?

I conclude on a note of the discriminations unexamined by those born to privilege using the vocabulary of the libertarians to challenge vocal protests of the Americans with Disabilities Act.[22] That protest focuses on government intrusion of private holdings inclusive of income garnered and business conducted. As libertarians argue, disability access beyond national, state, and local governments should be left to the "goodwill" and free choice of the owner. Thus, perpetuating the "tyranny of the normal,"[23] private schools would not be required to provide interpreters and wheelchair access, because those students could learn elsewhere or nowhere; new or renovating restaurants and shops would not have to admit the blind, the deaf, and wheelchair users, because those customers are not welcome; and businesses could refuse to hire people with disability, perpetuating the cycle of poverty that plagues most people with disability including those with the competencies and credentials needed to do the work for which they applied.

The problem with leaving support of accommodations to goodwill and charity leaves people with disability, their families, and their care-givers without security. Moreover, leaving this support to charity misses the critically important work of dismantling the systems that deny routine support to people with disability that remains operative under the assumptions of a purported inability to contribute to the social capital of the common good. Following Augustine on this point, "charity is no substitute for justice withheld."[24]

⚹ ⚹ ⚹

In sum, people with disability are more likely to have been denied the natural law ground of the common good means of developing their capabilities—to be, to love, to learn, to engage, to thrive—as a result of on-purpose denial by the dominant and others in authority with power or by their inadvertent failures to provide access. Ultimately, people with disability are as entitled as the nondisabled, if not preferentially so, to the goods of life, bodily health and inviolable integrity, education (in the realms of the senses, imagination, thought, emotions, and self-determination), intimate and social relationships, play, and a sustainable environment. In chapter 4 I turn to theological reflections on the *imago Dei* as the foundation of a theological anthropology of radical dependence and to the insights of the Catholic social teaching tradition on human dignity, participation, and solidarity.

— 4 —

Imago Dei, Theological Anthropology, and Catholic Social Teaching

I had a brother with Down syndrome who died suddenly in 2009. The year he passed, he had become an altar server, and for several months after his death a single alb remained draped over one empty server chair. I was told it was a tribute to him, an acknowledgment of a missing presence. I think about this image often when I think about inclusion in the Church—what power could it hold if we recognized how many other empty seats in our church truly belong to people with disabilities, lost not to death but to our failure to recognize that they belong there?

Lorraine Cuddeback-Gedeon

The underlying presuppositions of a Christian theological anthropology point to three matters of dogma: the revelation that God created human beings in God's own image, belief in Jesus of Nazareth as the Incarnate Word of God, and profession of faith in the Trinity. I take the Trinity—as a revelation of Divine Diversity—to be foundational to understanding the kind of being humankind images. In particular, I follow the tradition (from Jean Damascene to Karl Rahner, Catherine Mowry LaCugna, et al.) of Trinitarian *perichoresis*/circumincession as inherent relationality to be the key to understanding the inferences about the *imago Dei* human being and the subsequent necessary relationships between human persons "imaging" the *in se* and *ad extra* being of the Triune God.

Many have argued that the disciplines of theology are versions of or a kind of subspecies of anthropology.[1] That is, whatever we humans attempt to say about God reflects what we think is true about our-selves. However, where our theologies have asserted God's perfection as the basis of intellectual, physical, and gendered norms, those theologies have denied the full inheritance of the *imago Dei* to women, racialized and gendered others, and people with disability. The insights of these arguments about God's being and human being, though not their conclusions (many of which have marginalized women, people of color, gender diverse people, and people with disability), resonate with members of Christian communities who profess a revelation of the Incarnate God in the person of Jesus of Nazareth, the Risen Christ of Faith. And some Christians with disability find solace and affirmation in these insights, particularly insofar as Jesus—the Incarnate God, bro-ken, crucified, and glorified—reveals the marks of disability, with his hands and feet crippled by nails, his side pierced, and his face marred beyond human semblance,[2] without being stigmatized thereby for his disability. These insights about the Risen Christ lead to an anthropology that affirms people who do not conform to the ideologically and puta-tively normative perfections that oppress both the not-sick hail and the potentially sick frail[3] as well as the nondisabled and people with disabil-ity. Further, in this nonconformity, Nancy Eiesland discovers a theologi-cal anthropology of the disabled God.[4]

Unfortunately, most philosophical and theological anthropologies present a limited scope of "man" (as opposed to humankind), an ideal that very few attain. Black, feminist, Latinx and other context-based scholars have convinced most that the theo-philosophical traditions founded in classical Western and Enlightenment thought focus on things proper to white men almost singularly. Scholars in disability studies are in the process of convincing most that these same traditions focus on things proper to able-bodied, youthful, and robust men, with a small number of people ever attaining the ideal. The time has come to focus instead on things proper to and good for women, people of color, and people with disability and others considered to be "outliers" so as to increase the scope of the ideal to include the anthropological diversity of human beingness embodied in these heretofore invisible marginalized others. Thus, an ideal of anthropological diversity rejects the limiting notions that previously (and still) qualify being human to affirm instead that people with disability and others already attain this ideal.[5] Against these limitations in the tradition concerning who counts, Christians believe that the Triune God offers all creation the fullness of life, that all of creation was in the beginning and is now deemed good, and that human beings especially have a unique responsibility to care for one another as ambassadors of and for God.

An *Imago Dei* Theological Anthropology of Radical Dependence

That human beings can be ambassadors of God is a mystery, surely, and a revelation that suggests through an anthropological lens something about God in Godself (*in se*) and about God in creation (*ad extra*): God is unity in diversity. The doctrine of the Triune God considers that in God's very being, God is for others/God is for us.[6] With this understanding, gathered over time from the Christian experience of God in the world, the implications of the doctrine of the Trinity reveal relationality and relationship as the metaphysical ground of God's own being and all other beings as one or another expression of the *imago Dei*. This claim serves as the starting point of an anthropological paradigm shift from monad-like independence to relational dependence on others that distinguishes the diversity of being others in the world. The paradigm provides the immediacy of unity in diversity that both reveals God—as trirelational—and defines humankind, if not all of creation, as dependent-relational *imago Dei*. By God's own doing, the Divine Diversity of the Triune God present in the *imago Dei* is reflected in the kaleidoscopic diversity of being, including the diversity of disability present in humankind and in a planet subject to the forces of evolutionary and seismic change.[7]

In terms of theological anthropology, if God is three in one, then the implications of unity in diversity/diversity in unity extends to the *imago Dei*. In Trinitarian doctrine, God *intra/in se* (God in Godself) and God *ad extra* (God for Us) exposes the trirelational Christian faith in the one God. This doctrine is not a Christian pantheism; rather, since God became incarnate in the person of Jesus of Nazareth and remains active in the world through the Holy Spirit, God's self-revelation includes a tangible manifestation of the Divinity as unity in diversity, as the trirelational God communicating in love within/*in se* the Godhead and beyond/*ad extra* to creation. This relationality distinguishes the Persons of God as it reveals also the ways in which God acts in the world. As Christians, what we know about God is known through this relational Trinitarian lens. As Thomas Aquinas instructs, God's essence is the relationship that reveals the very being of God that is love known and outpoured.[8] We Christians know this Trinity—God the Father/Creator, God the Son/Incarnate Word of God, and God the Holy Spirit/Paraclete—through a lens manifest to us in the compelling early Church testimony of the Incarnation, Crucifixion, and Resurrection of Jesus along with the outpouring of the Holy Spirit then, since, and in our time. And through this lens we come to know something about ourselves, about our human beingness, as *imago Dei* relationality. Thus, if relationality built on a foundation of union-love characterizes God's unity in diversity, then relationality of a loving and liberatory sort must characterize human diversity present throughout the world.

A loving and liberatory relationality that images the Triune God in humankind belies the dualisms that artificially segregate one person from the main or one community from another. Rather than superficially observable physical/cognitive/emotional characteristics that seemingly divide people from one another (cf. Michel Foucault's norm-dividing practices), human anthropological diversity locates norms of being in relationships and communities that affirm human flourishing. Moving beyond a rather boring ideal—for instance, of the white heterosexual male—to the relationality that is a property of diversity transforms that putatively normative and idealized man of nondisabled fiction to all those outliers considered beyond the main: those deemed previously defective, less than, and disabled. Nancy Eiesland's insights on the disabled God are instructive. "The most astonishing fact is, of course, that Christians do not have an able-bodied God as their primal image. Rather, the Disabled God promising grace through a broken body is at the center of piety, prayer, practice, and mission."[9]

By way, then, of affirming the wide expression of humankind, the anthropological diversity presented by persons with disability may be uniquely indicative of human beingness. Further, I argue that this diversity exposes what is most true of human beings qua *imago Dei*: in order to be and to thrive, human beings must accept and affirm diversity as each one's relational dependence on as well as difference (i.e., distinction) between one another. "In presenting his impaired body to his startled friends, the resurrected Jesus is revealed as the disabled God. . . . [H]ere was the resurrected Christ making good on the promise that God would be with us, embodied, as we are—disabled and divine."[10] Relational dependence reveals human unity in diversity; as such, dependence of the kind required for the support of human lives holds liberative normative force for humankind.[11] As a dynamic force, this norm requires nothing less than affirmation of every person regardless of their race, gender, or ability and, to the extent that they have been denied, the explicit, intentional, and robust affirmation of persons with disability of every and any kind.[12] The *imago Dei* title that God bestowed on Earth's first human creatures and all humankind thereafter and the Trinitarian image of God revealed to us in Jesus must be admitted as none other than the right realization of our mutual needs, our dependence on one another, and our care that each will flourish and thrive.[13] However, unlike the trirelational unity-in-diversity that is God simply and God freely for us, relational diversity in humankind is radical and dependent.

The paradigm shift toward diversity in a theological anthropology of relationality begs consideration of relationship(s) with whom, why, and how. It is to Catholic social teaching that I look for ways that answer these questions. In particular, I focus here on the themes of human dignity, solidarity, and the promotion of peace through a Catholic and an interdenominational World Council of Churches mission lens to raise the quality of life for people on the physical and proverbial margins,[14] In chapter 5, I explore Catholic social teaching on participation and the preferential option for the poor as the means through which a preferential justice for people with disability may be realized.

The Church's Work for Human Dignity, Solidarity, and the Promotion of Peace

Many have recognized the relevance of the Catholic Church to, for, and with people who are or have been beyond the scope of interest, inexperienced in the drive for power, and marginal to a hegemonic agenda of normativity—these are the people who stand literally and figuratively outside of the community of the faithful. Surprisingly or not, mission initiatives historically have spread from a center—for example, from Jerusalem, Rome, Antioch, and capital cities elsewhere—to a periphery, the proverbial ends of the earth. Today, however, the concept of mission evangelization has shifted from a starting place at those centers to a starting place by those at the periphery and margins of their cultures and purported communities: the new evangelizing witnesses to the Good News of salvation found in liberation theology. These evangelizers transform the ways in which those who have held their places at the center now come to see God's liberating spirit in the world form the edges, where the big-picture view of goings-on can be observed.[15] More than a reverse mission concept (where those to whom people with privilege go "to serve and to evangelize the less fortunate" find themselves served and evangelized instead), this shift signals a radical reappraisal of God's own mission in the world: human flourishing for all—and arguably in particular for those whose means to flourish have been compromised—inclusive of the implications of support for all of creation. Evangelization today returns to or reasserts the original dignity bestowed on humankind as *imago Dei*. If the Church is to cooperate with God's mission today, it is necessary for every community to establish solidarity with and inclusion of all God's people: with every instance of the *imago Dei* in humankind and, given the abusive past they have experienced, solidarity especially with those on the margins and the many others who have been denigrated by the powers and their minions for their presumed "less than desirable" presence in God's house.[16] The Church cannot afford to do otherwise.

Arguably, the principles of human dignity, solidarity, and the promotion of peace can be addressed under the single call to respect for the dignity inherent in each person as *imago Dei*. No other qualification or specification of worth beyond *imago Dei* dignity is really necessary to challenge and inspire the faithful in regard to care with and for one another to build thereby a world where peace and flourishing prevail. Nevertheless, reminders of the root of human dignity, the companionship and accompaniment of solidarity, and the right relationship in social affairs and equity as matters for the work of social justice and the promotion of peace are necessary.

As the *Compendium of the Social Doctrine of the Church* instructs on the equal dignity of all people and with particular reference to people with disability,

(144) *Since something of the glory of God shines on the face of every person, the dignity of every person before God is the basis of the dignity of [a human being] before other [human beings]* [cf. Vatican II, *Gaudium et spes*, §29]. Moreover, this is the ultimate foundation of the radical equality and [kinship] among all people, regardless of their race, nation, sex, origin, culture, or class.

(145) *Only the recognition of human dignity can make possible the common and personal growth of everyone* (cf. Jas 2:1-9). To stimulate this kind of growth it is necessary in particular to help the least, effectively ensuring conditions of equal opportunity for men and women and guaranteeing an objective equality between the different social classes before the law [cf. Paul VI, *Octogesima Adveniens*, §16].

(148) *Persons with disabilities are fully human subjects, with rights and duties*: "in spite of the limitations and sufferings affecting their bodies and faculties, they point up more clearly the dignity and greatness of [humankind]" [John Paul II, *Laborem Exercens*, §22]. Since persons with disabilities are subjects with all their rights, they are to be helped to participate in every dimension of family and social life at every level accessible to them and according to their possibilities.

The rights of persons with disabilities need to be promoted with effective and appropriate measures: "It would be radically unworthy of [humankind], and a denial of our common humanity, to admit to the life of the community, and thus admit to work, only those who are fully functional. To do so would be to practice a serious form of discrimination, that of the strong and healthy against the weak and sick" [John Paul II, *Laborem Exercens*, §22]. Great attention must be paid not only to the physical and psychological work conditions, to a just wage, to the possibility of promotion and the elimination of obstacles, but also to the affective and sexual dimensions of persons with disabilities: "They too need to love and to be loved, they need tenderness, closeness and intimacy" [John Paul II, "Message for the International Symposium on the Dignity and Rights of the Mentally Disabled Person," 1/4/2004], according to their capacities and with respect for the moral order, which is the same for [those with disability and the nondisabled] alike.[17]

Along with other scriptural, catechetical, and human rights terms found throughout the *Compendium*, this instruction confirms the dignity of all persons and the protections of opportunities that belong to each.

Still, at this moment of increased consciousness concerning the widespread vulnerability of individuals and communities across the globe, God calls for a collective commitment to the future where the past is admitted, lament is expressed, and the dangerous memories of Jesus's passion and of the untold neglected multitude of others' deaths is redeemed not by their sufferings but instead by a now and future peace.[18] A future that values the *imago Dei* must interrupt now the Empire and those who have wielded their power recklessly so as to unveil new and dangerous insights for the present. The danger reveals failures and sin, while the insights foretell the work of dismantling oppression to collaborate in God's mission designs for humankind.[19] Moreover, as those insights come now from people on the periphery, from those who witness the Good News of liberation that God is for us, the relevance of our churches depends on partnerships in mission with them. Contrary to the Empire's will to power, by living and acting together in mission—accommodating, affirming, and advocating for and with one another—we will champion diversity as God's own fecund imaginary, we will celebrate dependence as the nature of human being—*imago Dei*, and in the places of commerce and political power as well as of the Eucharist and dinner, we will share worship, friendship, and right relationship.

In this work of dismantling overt and covert oppressions, peace grows. As Paul VI taught, "If you want Peace, work for Justice."[20] In "Peace: The Fruit of Justice and Love," the *Compendium of the Social Doctrine of the Church* instructs further that

> (494) *Peace is not merely the absence of war, nor can it be reduced solely to the maintenance of a balance of power between enemies* [cf. *Gaudium et spes*, §78]. *Rather it is founded on a correct understanding of the human person* [cf. John Paul II, *Centesimus Annus*, §51] *and requires the establishment of an order based on justice and charity.*

> *Peace is the fruit of justice* [cf. Paul VI, Message for the 1972 World Day of Peace] (cf. Is 32:17) understood in the broad sense as the respect for the equilibrium of every dimension of the human person. Peace is threatened when [a human being] is not given all that is due [each] as a human person, when [the *imago Dei*] dignity is not respected and when civil life is not directed to the common good. The defense and promotion of human rights is essential for the building up of a peaceful society and the integral development of individuals, peoples and nations [cf. Paul VI, Message for the 1969 World Day of Peace].[21]

As the *Compendium* corresponds with the work of the World Council of Churches, the Catholic Church is concerned for people on the margins. Among other Catholic service agencies, Caritas Internationalis shares the mission of the Church "to serve the poor and to promote charity and justice throughout the world. . . . Caritas promotes integral human development so that people in the worst off and most disadvantaged communities are free to flourish and live in peace and dignity."[22] Caritas embodies the work of peace with justice by saving lives, responding to natural and human-caused disasters, promoting integral human development to facilitate survival, and recovery from crises so as to live and thrive in peace. In particular, Caritas regions in Armenia, Australia, Austria, Bulgaria, Egypt, Germany, and Shqiptar/Albania specifically identify people with disability as part of their work to end poverty, promote justice, and uphold each person's dignity. Caritas Australia too is emphatic: "disability is both a cause and a consequence of poverty, and therefore we ensure that all community development programs are accessible to people with disabilities . . . and empower them to actively participate in community development and decision making activities so that they are architects of their own development."[23] These regions provide necessary aid that supports global Caritas initiatives of development, strengthening health services and educational or vocational programs to children and adults with disability in need, and protecting them from a downward spiral into poverty.

The practical theological foundations of this outreach rest in the traditions of the universal Church. Much praise can be offered to the Church for its teachings and the consistency of its message on the sanctity of all human life as well as its dependence on God's good creation (given global environmental degradation, this dependence is appreciated more today than in the past)[24] and God's continued intervention in human affairs. Although it may have seemed that God was not watching, perhaps something related to the Holocaust and its vicious pogrom against the Jewish people and against people with disability inspired John XXIII in 1963 to acknowledge people with disability in his peace encyclical, *Pacem in Terris*.[25] John XXIII named the rights accorded to all people across exigencies whenever they present throughout a life span: the right to life, education, work, shelter, and other necessary social services that may be needed on account of ill health, disability, or loss of livelihood.[26] With the papacy of John Paul II, sustained and explicit concern for people with disability and their integration into all arenas of society was raised for the Catholic faithful and for all of the world to observe; his successors, Benedict XVI and Francis, have noted

perseverance in the face of adversities by persons with disability, thanked
those who advocate on their behalf, and stood themselves as witnesses
to encountering, being in solidarity with, and including people with disability.[27] Pope Francis continues to advocate for the inclusion of people
with disability and to encourage the faithful with and without disability
to love and to persevere.[28]

Certainly, the Church has a stake in the care of, for, and with persons
and communities of people with disability as much as it has a stake in
the care of, for, and with the nondisabled. More than care, the Church
suggests (almost) a theology for disability in its preparatory documents
for the year 2000/third millennium celebrations' Jubilee Day of the Community with Persons with Disabilities. Those documents start with a
treatise titled "The Person with Disabilities: The Image of God and a
Place of His Wonders." Although the language of this start strikes many,
rightly, as patronizing for its identification of persons with disability as a
manifestation of God's wonders, as if such persons are given to the nondisabled for their edification or upon whom they can bestow charity,
the treatise concludes with the challenge to "conversion and to discernment of Gospel values" of inclusion.[29] Further, the Preparatory Committee asserts that "the person with disabilities is rich in humanity,"[30]
"has every right to be a subject-active agent in ministry,"[31] and "has
every right to be a subject-receiver of evangelization and catechesis,"[32]
concluding that "the person with disabilities has rights and duties like
every other individual."[33] Again, the deliberate reference to being "rich
in humanity" suggests a patronizing something "special" or above
the inspirational norm that signals fundamental differences between
persons with disability and the nondisabled. Valorization of this sort
betrays a kind of paternalist prejudice and insulting thereby as it rein-
forces perceptions among the nondisabled of a lack of agency on the
part of persons with disability.[34] As Nancy Eiesland cautions, "As long
as disability is unaddressed theologically or addressed only as a 'special
interest perspective,' the Christian church will continue to propagate a
double-minded stance that holds up the disabled as objects of ministry and adulation for overcoming the very barriers that the church has
helped to construct."[35] With an important turn from this posture, Pope

Francis goes further in the 2017 Vatican conference "Catechesis and Persons with Disabilities: A Necessary Engagement in the Pastoral Life of the Church." There Francis referred to liberation theology insights on marginalization and focused on inclusion, solidarity, and participation with the "hope that more and more people with disabilities can become catechists themselves in their communities, offering their own witness and helping to communicate the faith more effectively."[36] Eiesland argues further that "any theology that seeks access for people with disabilities must necessarily come from a liberatory voice that continues to be constituted by a dialogue within the community of people with disabilities that locate us at the speaking center," an unequivocal way to avoid the snares of past practice.[37]

In 1978, the United States Conference of Catholic Bishops (USCCB) issued "Pastoral Statement on Persons with Disabilities" wherein it recognized the Church's obligations to safeguard the Body of Christ, particularly in the sacraments, and to build the Kingdom of God's peace and love:

The Catholic Church pursues its mission by furthering the spiritual, intellectual, moral and physical development of the people it serves. As pastors of the Church in America, we are committed to working for a deeper understanding of both the pain and the potential of our neighbors who are blind, deaf, mentally retarded, emotionally impaired, who have special learning problems, or who suffer from single or multiple physical handicaps—all those whom disability may set apart. We call upon people of good will to reexamine their attitudes toward their brothers and sisters with disabilities and [to] promote their well-being, acting with the sense of justice and the compassion that the Lord so clearly desires.[38]

The USCCB remains attentive to the ongoing need for actions designed intentionally to advocate for ministry to and with people with disability. In 1995, combining canon law with sacramental theology, the USCCB's 1978 "Pastoral Statement," and insights from the corpus of John Paul II and other Vatican offices, it published "Guidelines for the Celebration of the Sacraments with Persons with Disabilities."[39] (To the

USCCB's credit, the Vatican Committee for the year 2000 Jubilee Day masses adopted these guidelines for the community of people with disability who attended the third millennium Jubilee events.) The hermeneutic key for these guidelines is access to full sacramental participation by Catholic persons and communities of people with disability across the diverse landscapes of the US Church, from urban to suburban and rural dioceses to parishes staffed by diocesan or religious order priests. "Catholics with disabilities have a right to participate in the sacraments as fully as other members of the local ecclesial community."[40]

Again, as the *Compendium* builds its case from the principle of participation and the social nature of humankind, the principle of solidarity comes to the fore:

(192) Solidarity highlights in a particular way the intrinsic social nature of the human person, the equality of all in dignity and rights and the common path of individuals and peoples towards an ever more committed unity. Never before has there been such a widespread awareness of the bond of interdependence between individuals and peoples, which is found at every level.

In the presence of the phenomenon of interdependence and its constant expansion, however, there persist in every part of the world stark inequalities between developed and developing countries, inequalities stoked also by various forms of exploitation, oppression and corruption that have a negative influence on the internal and international life of many States. *The acceleration of interdependence between persons and peoples needs to be accompanied by equally intense efforts on the ethical-social plane,* in order to avoid the dangerous consequences of perpetrating injustice on a global scale. This would have very negative repercussions even in the very countries that are presently more advantaged [John Paul II, *Sollicitudo Rei Socialis*, §11-22].[41]

All things considered, officially the Catholic Church is dedicated to people with disability in the same ways it is dedicated to all the faithful.

Unfortunately, a practical reality of exclusion remains true for persons with disability and other members of the Catholic communion (e.g., gender, racial/ethnic, and language minorities) who continue to be marginalized if not by physical obstacles then by prejudices, discriminations, and ignorance. Many local churches are quite inaccessible, unwelcoming, and disvaluing of the diversity presented in the ecclesia by persons with disability. These failures reflect a patronizing lip service to "all are welcome" where solidarity and visible inclusion ought to prevail. For example, many churches were built decades before the consciousness raising of civil rights pertaining to people with disability; as such, many of these churches include steps to their entrances, effectively leaving people with mobility impairments shut out of the assembly, their access to religious rites denied for all intents and purposes unless a ramp is installed as an alternative passage to the sanctuary. As long as entryways remain inaccessible, the Church is consciously or not indicating a virtual unwelcoming "No Service" sign for people with mobility impairments. While the architects and builders of those earlier days should not be faulted, it is disheartening that so many of these building entrances have not yet been adapted to accommodate access to the physical structures that at present obstruct the way for those who want to enter. Related to the physical barriers, persons who are or have become homebound as a result of debilitating conditions and who appreciate the visits of a priest or minister to their homes will still miss the Sunday and other holy day gatherings of the community that is the Church. Communication technologies today could remedy some of the isolation experienced by many parishioners who would be accommodated with, for example, services of the Church gathered that could be livestreamed between the building and their homes (since the COVID-19 pandemic shut down worship spaces, many churches scrambled to equip their liturgical spaces with this technology; post-pandemic, streaming could continue effortlessly). Entryway stairs and homebound isolation are just two examples that demonstrate where the local ecclesial community has failed not only the USCCB's and popes' directives on inclusion but also, perhaps more importantly, the people who desire the sacramental graces and friendships otherwise available in the universal Church. Other examples of accessible accommodations include hearing induction loops, sign interpretation, and plain or simplified liturgical spaces, sights, and sounds. These accessibility initiatives are visible signs of solidarity and participation—as opposed to "Not Welcome" signs—on the part of the community to embrace its members with disability.

For positive change, the resources developed by the National Catholic Partnership on Disability with and for persons with disability and their families are both helpful and hopeful. These resources provide practical help and suggestions on a spectrum of services including advocacy initiatives for parish outreach, concerns related to ministry with and for people with specific kinds of disability, assistance for priests and lay ministers with vision impairments, and information on accessible design and redesign. Finally, these resources emphasize across-the-board collaboration and the integration of persons and communities of people with disability in ministry whereby the Church's mission will be fulfilled. The partnership adapts the principles of architectural universal design[42] to a "universally designed ministry" that offers the aims of inclusion as coterminus with the call to discipleship that characterizes the People of God.[43] Its *Opening Doors to Welcome* follows the theological insights on the *imago Dei* and Catholic social teaching on human dignity, the preferential option, and solidarity; additionally, *Opening Doors to Welcome* recognizes the practical challenges of orchestrating any liturgical celebrations with a view to noting how such celebrations can embody the hospitable reach of Jesus's own sharing of touch in the communion that is his Body, the Church,[44] as well as the communion of Eucharist, the source and summit of Christian life.[45]

I conclude this chapter with a caution.

We have it on fairly certain grounds—from none other than Jesus and attested to by the Spirit at Pentecost (Acts 2:1–12)—that heaven/God's house is welcoming to people (and all of creation) from every tribe, race, gender, tongue, and ability in the world. I wonder about the implications of the arduous work of becoming an inclusive community. Difficulties will be encountered in meeting the challenges of accommodating, affirming, and advocating with and for people belonging to tribes, races, genders, languages, and abilities that are different from the local familiar and hegemonically normative. However, to do anything else at this moment of critical consciousness is to act contrary to God's hospitality and mission designs for the world. I am concerned too that a very great number of people in ages past and still today have been refused entry into communities of friendship and of worship, especially the communities to which many of us belong and where we proclaim Jesus as Lord and Savior. Many of these/our communities and their/our leaders will have much explaining to do when the Spirit of truth and love asks, "Why did you not make a way?" Or in turn when they ask, "When, Lord, did we see you hungry, thirsty, naked, sick, estranged, or imprisoned?" (Mt 25: 31–46) or, for lack of access, were locked out of the assembly. Ignorance in failing to take note of who is not present— and why—may not save those who will be deemed culpable.

✻ ✻ ✻

In order to move from neglect of people with disability to affirmation and advocacy, it is necessary to uncover what has been heretofore hidden from mainstream understanding, namely that people with disability are people first! People are made in God's image and likeness. Diversity is the complexion of creation, and dependence is the essential and radical character of humankind; any disadvantaging discrimination and oppression against any person therefore exposes the contour of sin against God and neighbor. Accommodations are the minimum expected from this moment forward. Affirmation of people with disability will include recognition of diversity in creation inclusive of the diversity across the spectrum of ability as well as the dependence that is the reality of all humankind upon the webs of relationships that beget, befriend, and support each and every one of us. And advocacy with and for people with disability will reflect the principles of human dignity, solidarity, and peace with justice indicative of the revelation that is the Crucified God, Jesus of Nazareth, the Risen Disabled Christ of Faith.

— 5 —

A Preferential Justice for Those Who Are Poor or Otherwise Marginalized

There's nothing preferential about preferential justice. It simply affords me, as a person with disability, the same access to opportunities to live well, thrive, grow, and love that people without disabilities take for granted. Jesus welcomed Bartimaeus when others would stifle the would-be disciple's call. Preferential justice is the way that we answer Jesus's call to do the same.

Maria Cataldo-Cunniff

The incorporation of a liberation theology hermeneutic into the official corpus of Catholic social teaching may be surprising, given the Church's stance against a fretful intrusion of Marxist ideologies that may jeopardize religious liberty with a revolution built on conscientization regarding the roots of poverty, dependency, and exploitation. However, this incorporation is also not surprising given the Church's mandate from Jesus to "go and do likewise" in service to and solidarity with one another, especially with those who have been abused on account of their difference from the main. We are called to relieve the distress of those who are poor as a result of the abuse and neglect they suffer at the hands of the mighty (Lk 10:25–37) and to meet the critical needs of persons regardless of which tribe (Samaritan or Black, Hispanic/Latinx, Asian, Arab, non-Christian, poor, or disabled) they hail from.[1]

Having considered how the principles of human dignity, solidarity, and the promotion of peace can inform the imperatives of inclusion concerning people with disability, I begin this chapter with acceptance of liberationist insights regarding God's preferential mission to people with disability as a community on the margins, outside the Church, deemed less than desirable, in short, as people from another tribe. With a liberationist interrogation into the meaning of "the poor," it is obvious that God's preferential option applies to people with disability, who are often very materially poor and otherwise marginalized on account of their vulnerability to and experience of being othered in prankish and vicious ways as well as poor in a lack of advocates and friends. Liberation theologies illuminate how God is the champion of those who are oppressed and otherwise marginalized.[2]

Some progress engaging the preferential option has been made on behalf of people with disability and others who have been marginalized.[3] While more women, more racialized minority persons, and more gender-diverse persons have claimed their places in their communities of birth, schools, work, and worship, a very great number of people with disability in ages past and still today continue to be refused entry into communities of friendship and other relational potentials. In addition, conditions of material poverty among people who have been marginalized remain extreme (nearly one billion living on less than two dollars per day!).[4] In these ways of being refused, people with disability have in the past and still typify today those who are marginalized in the contemporary world. The refusal to abandon marginalizing others on the part of Christian communities in particular is nothing less than scandalous in a tradition that holds all humankind in every instance as having been created in God's own image and likeness. Justice demands that persons with disability and others who are marginalized receive their due preferentially, especially since what's due is what has been denied them in spite of their personhood as *imago Dei*. That denial is sinful. In order to reverse the sin, justice demands that they have access to all the conditions necessary for their flourishing in the fullness of life with all due haste. This way of conceptualizing the preferential option—as a preferential justice—returns to the subject matter, insights, and demands of natural law and the common good and reminds us of the dangers that come with a just and subversive love.

If diversity is God's own calling card—both in Trinitarian doctrine and visible widely in creation—then an affirmation of diversity, particularly the diversity in humankind inclusive of people with disability, is an affirmation of God in the created order and a cause for thanks and praise. To the extent that people with disability represent a significantly large cohort of the human population (15–20 percent or more) and to the extent that their normative diversity—widespread, diverse in kind, and nondiscriminatory—is uniquely the common denominator indicative of being human, diversity signals God's fecund imaginary as it was in the beginning, is now, and ever will be. What then are we the people and we the churches/the Body of Christ to do to become communities worthy of God's image and likeness? How may we disengage exclusionary practices and engage the hard work and high cost—especially the cost of reimagining and reenvisioning millennia-held assumptions about norms—of accommodating diversity? When will welcoming, affirming, and integrating persons and communities of people with disability in the assembly be realized (how long must your people with disability wait, O Lord)? What revisions to existing physical, attitudinal, and philosophical structures and their systemic-institutionalized supports are required to reverse the neglect (and worse) that persons with disability have suffered? What imperative force does a theological anthropology of radical dependence hold for a people who fashion their norms for what it means to be *imago Dei* in a disabled God?

What more? Political will is an important though insufficient step, as evidence of compliance or the lack thereof with the Americans with Disabilities Act reveals.[5] Many hearts and minds are yet in need of metanoia if systemic-institutionalized ableism is to lose its power to marginalize and oppress the People of God. And intentional relationships are yet to be formed across the spectrum of being human in a world where fecund asymmetry and creative imaginary are celebrated according to the mission designs of the Holy Trinity *in se* and God for us *ad extra*. Nothing less than a preferential relationship, ideally a friendship, will do.

Justice for People with Disability

Nothing less than relationship will do. "In the *kenosis* of the Incarnation and in the disabling of the Crucifixion, God definitively entered into solidarity with humankind."[6] That solidarity—God's identification with the diversity of creation in humankind—centers on the relationality that Christians understand to be the way God is in relation with Godself, in the Trinitarian relations of God-Father, God-Son, and God-Spirit *in se*, and in relation with us, the *imago Dei* human being and all of creation *ad extra*. Reflection on the "disabled God" reveals that human life and mortality become—by God's own kenotic self-emptying into humanity through gestational embodiment and birth to childhood and adulthood to crucifixion and death—the experience of God in Godself and God for us, as God with us in the person of Jesus of Nazareth and in the presence of the Holy Spirit throughout. In Jesus, God and the *imago Dei* of humankind are united in unmediated solidarity and intimate friendship. The Incarnation reveals God definitively for and with us over the centuries and, however obliquely, God for us in the proclamation of the Good News that Christians have given witness to Jesus since. Christians witness Jesus, whose very humanity was resurrected with disability without his being oppressed to confirm his identity (see Jn 20:24–29 where the resurrected Jesus directs the Apostle Thomas to touch the evidence of his wounds); Jesus, whose relations *in se* within the Trinity and relations *ad extra* for us remain intact; and Jesus, by whom God is glorified.[7] With Jesus of Nazareth, the Incarnate Word of God, God demonstrates a preference (as far as any of us can know) for humankind.

Thus, if diversity is God's calling card and the Incarnation is the expression of God's mission designs for all of creation, then justice making must be the hallmark medium—God's means of self-communication—of the Good News in our churches and beyond. Our all-too-feeble ways of conceiving God's designs fall woefully short in recognizing diversity as God's own fecund imaginary that makes "solidarity with"—the quintessential paradigmatic norm for relationality—the way that people are to be with people. Yet, the failure to recognize diversity parallels the thinking that the cross on which God Incarnate hung in preferential solidarity with all people who are oppressed is folly. Nevertheless, Christians believe in that folly (cf. 1 Cor 1:18–25) even as we ask how it can be that God so loved the world that God in Jesus delivered Godself, preferentially, to the vulnerability and to the joys of being human as well as to the vulnerability and to the vicissitudes of human sin and evil, the vulnerability to be accounted a sinner and accursed, and the vulnerability to suffer the executioners' cross. That accounting and suffering continues to confound human understanding of God's mission designs as still we fail to assent to God's own designated kenosis and preferential vulnerability.

Consider, in the fullness of that time—from the Annunciation to Mary, Joseph's dream and Jesus's humble birth, modest childhood, itinerant ministry, and torturous demise—God Incarnate suffered the extremes of mortality as experienced by the multitudes before and since. That Incarnate solidarity witnessed definitively, once and for all, God's preferential option for those who are poor and otherwise marginalized or oppressed. Moreover, Jesus's own life and teaching challenges every hegemony, norm, and ideology that presumes some are better than most and that those accounted as the least do not matter much at all (cf. Lk 9:46–48). Christians today must likewise challenge that hegemonic normativity regarding who counts in witness to God's preferences and mission designs; we must embrace diversity and engage friendships in solidarity as Jesus has invited us to do (those on the outside will know that we are Christians by our love for one another; cf. Jn 13:34–35). Those friendships, that solidarity, and the preferential love that we have for one another will then be the medium by which our churches proclaim and witness ever more genuinely the Good News. Actions speak louder than words: our relevance as the Catholic Church depends on the risk and the scandal of the Incarnation; the alternative may be a decision to forget the project altogether and "close the doors."[8]

If God is for us and if in Jesus that "for us" overflows into friendship and solidarity with humankind, then friendship and solidarity must mark—not in stigmatizing but rather in liberating ways of advocacy— each Christian and every church. Many Christians have become ever more aware of people at the margins, including people with disability.[9] That awareness presents itself as a growing consciousness of the perversions that are human designs for power over and sin against those who are vulnerable. And that sin is expressed throughout the pages of the dominant narrative: the marginalization and oppression of people deemed "other," a persistent human hubris against God and one another, and the outright rejection of God's designs of liberation for all humankind. From that consciousness, giving witness to the disabled God means that Christians take care of one another and will preferentially take care of persons who are vulnerable nearby and across the globe. "It is the role of the church in this new century to face the reality of humanity in the image of a disabled Jesus; [that is, face] the reality of people with disabilities who are rejected and abandoned."[10] Those realities were exposed in the history and its residual legacy of oppression directed against persons with disability from antiquity to the present. Inconsistent with the God of pathos and love, with the God who prefers the company of those who are marginalized or otherwise oppressed, many of us and our churches have been complacent in ignoring the realities and experiences of people with disability today, and some (many?) have been complicit as well in contributing to their rejection and abandonment.

Contrary to a history of oppression toward people with disability, Catholic social teaching insists on the dignity belonging to all persons, the imperatives associated with human relationality, and on radical dependence extant in humankind. I want to push the principle of an option for the poor beyond its homiletic meaning to hortatory action for justice preferentially with and for people with disability. The paradigm shift toward diversity in an *imago Dei* theological anthropology of relationality and radical dependence begs consideration of relationship(s) with whom, why, and how?

Regardless of where our lives began, since our conceptions and births each of us is relationally dependent on others: mothers, fathers, siblings, extended family members, and friends as well as church, school, work, play, commerce, social services, infrastructure, and so on. Many—and surely most of those whose luck it was to be raised in privileged contexts—take these relational dependencies and access to the common good for granted. However, for those whose luck was not as favorably privileged—those who are poor, marginalized, and vulnerable thereby to the vicissitudes of invisibility and poverty—church, school, work, play, and services are neither readily accessible nor easily taken for granted.[11] As the United Nations and its global partners demonstrate in commitments that arise from the Jewish, Christian, and Muslim traditions, secular institutions are leading the way on inclusion (this lead ought to be considered an embarrassment for the Catholic Church). Accessibility is key to both inclusion and participation. One of the metrics in the WHO's *International Classification of Functioning and Disability* involves determinations of the levels of participation that persons with disability enjoy or lack. Success requires naming the obvious obstacles (awareness of which is often missed by the nondisabled) that mitigate participation.[12] Then, to increase participation, remove structural and attitudinal societal hindrances and provide social supports and facilitators so as to make participation of any sort easily accessible to all who so desire it.

With whom are people with disability in relationship? Hopefully, at minimum, persons with disability experience relationships within their families of birth although that is not always the case, as the histories of their oppression to the contemporary histories of institutionalization or worse—abortion, experimentation, and euthanasia—reveal. Even so, family and other intimate relationships for many persons with disability can be precarious, especially when personal care is needed: persons with disability are more likely to experience domestic violence than the nondisabled.[13] Education, employment, and recreation where friendships often form have been similarly difficult for people with disability to access.[14] Nevertheless, a preferential option for relationships across the diversity divide presents opportunities for all to thrive—a community, like a chain, is only as strong as its least-advantaged members even when those members are marginalized with impunity.

Why does a theological anthropology of radical dependence present an imperative to accepting and seeking intentional relationships with others seemingly "not like us," and why should "we" care? The simple answer is that not a single one of us human beings is so like another that each of us could be confused with another or that there are no distinctions among us. It is folly to think that creation in its innumerable forms and function is uniform. As noted in chapter 1's attention to norm making and in chapter 4's attention to a Trinitarian theological anthropology of diversity, in the world of mutual relationality diversity in humankind—itself kaleidoscopic in form and fecund asymmetry even in disability—is the sine qua non norm of relationality. The theological answer presents the scandal of kenosis, God-deigned-incarnate-solidarity, as an exceedingly intentional relationship with humankind including the scandal of crucifixion: the ultimate othering in antiquity[15] and comparable to the kinds of othering persons and communities of people with disability endure still.

How are such intentional relationships to be formed? The challenges that Christians face globally in meeting the demands of relational solidarity to the depths that Jesus exemplifies may be insurmountable; nevertheless, in whatever ways they may unfold, those relationships will vary in kind and from place to place. Moreover, in wanting to be known as his disciples, Christians must find a way to be in relationship with one another and make time to become friends.[16] Because people with disability have been excluded from the places of common intercourse, those who are nondisabled must make a preferential option to go to where persons and communities of people with disability may be and, in that going, go not just once or twice (as a service project, for example) but regularly. You have to show up reliably to be a friend and to be recognized by another as a friend. Like the stages of life, relationships with friends take time to develop and even more time to thrive. Additionally, the demands of kenotic relational solidarity require participatory inclusion. In imitation of Christ, all Christians need to adjust their approach to others with a posture of humility/self-sacrifice/kenosis and respect. "At its core, [kenosis is] the key reference point of Christian discipleship and ethical discernment."[17]

Further, Christians are called to do more, to be disposed to others and disposed preferentially toward those who have not been readily accommodated to participate in community. As an example, in advance of the Great Jubilee 2000 Jubilee Day of the Community of Persons with Disabilities, the Preparatory Committee provided a position paper for those who would be responsible for moving the agenda of the Church toward understanding and appreciation of people with disability who would travel to Vatican City for the December 3, 2000, program and beyond:

Disability is not a punishment, it is a place where normality and stereotypes are challenged and the Church and society are moved to search for that crucial point at which the human person is fully [herself/zirself/]himself.[18]

This paper aims to help discover that the person with disability is a privileged interlocutor of society and the Church.

It is in this spirit that we entrust this preparation to all of you, in view of the full integration and inclusion of persons with disabilities in the life of the Church and to society, to valorise [recognize] the gifts they bring, to reconcile ourselves with them for failings in their regard in the spirit of the Great Jubilee and to encourage an attitude of caring, assistance, and solidarity.[19]

Seven years and two popes later, the 2017 Vatican Conference "Catechesis and Persons with Disabilities: A Necessary Engagement in the Daily Pastoral Life of the Church" witnessed continued commitment to and development in the hierarchy's understanding of the rights of persons with disability to grow in Christian faith and to participate in the life of the Church. As Archbishop Rino Fisichella, president of the Pontifical Council for Promoting the New Evangelization, remarked on the opening day of the conference, the Catholic Church "must learn how to encounter disabled people today, how to allow them to have an encounter with Christ in the silence of their own interior . . . ; how to foster their witness and to be protagonists in the community as catechists, and therefore believers who transmit the faith, living it, and teaching it."[20] For Fisichella and the participants at the conference, "the topic of disability within the Christian community is urgent." Pope Francis rejoins similarly:

We recognize the great development there has been over the course of recent decades with regard to disability. Greater awareness of the dignity of each person, especially of the weakest, has led to the espousal of courageous positions for the inclusion of those who live with various forms of handicap [disability], so that no one should feel like a stranger in [her/zir/]his own home. Yet, at the cultural level, through a prevailing false understanding of life, expressions that harm the dignity of these persons still persist. . . . In the common mindset, there is still too strong an attitude of *rejection of this condition*, as if it prevents one from achieving happiness and self-fulfillment. . . . In reality, we know many people who, despite even serious fragility, have found, albeit with difficulty, the path of a good life, rich in meaning. . . . [It] is a perilous deception to think we are invulnerable. As said by a girl whom I met on my recent journey to Colombia: "vulnerability is intrinsic to the essential nature of [humankind]."

. . . The Church cannot be voiceless or out of tune in the defense and promotion of people with disabilities. Her closeness to the families helps them to overcome the loneliness that often risks closing them off for want of attention and support. This [risk] applies even more so due to her responsibility with regard to generating and forming the Christian life. The community must not lack the words and above all the gestures for encountering and welcoming people with disabilities. . . .

Catechesis, in a particular way, is called to discover and test congruent forms so that each [and every] person, with their gifts, limitations and even severe disabilities, can encounter Jesus on their journey and trustfully abandon themselves to Him. No physical or mental limitation could ever be an impediment to this encounter, because Christ's face shines in the heart of each person. . . .

Lastly, I hope that in the community, more and more people with disabilities may be their own catechists, by their witness too, so as to pass on the faith in a more effective way.[21]

These efforts are more than promising for persons with disability in the Church, especially as the institution begins to realize both a historically paternalist tendency to want to do for others what they can do for themselves and its increasing awareness of structural and attitudinal barriers to full inclusion that will only come about through the participation of and catechizing by persons with disability themselves in the ecclesia.

Practically, many wonder about the costs and dangers of moving forward. Further, the work of full participatory inclusion can be uncomfortably disruptive for the nondisabled. Compare the difficulties encountered while moving an institution (or a nation) and its culture from a racially segregated past to a future of integration: the civil rights movement in the United States presents one challenging example of the struggles of normalizing—of making regular—the participation of people with disability throughout the main instead of in the margins.[22] Still, it is clear that the Church of the twenty-first century desires to be inclusive.[23]

Notwithstanding this desire, becoming a Church that is fully inclusive of all and in all levels of its structures will require more than a few days of conferencing with, about, and for people with disability: it will require a commitment of resources and personnel minimally for education on disability and architecturally on reconfiguring worship and community space. As many wait for that justice in the meantime, what words of liberation are to be spoken for those who have been bowed down and oppressed on account of disability? Who is responsible for raising the consciences and the consciousness of Christians and others unfamiliar with this largest global minority of people in recognizing the absence of persons with disability in our communities, in our families, and as our friends? When will solidarity be embraced as a support for and way to be in those friendships? How much longer must people with disability wait for the Church to repair the damage of the oppressions that our siblings with disability have experienced across time (after all, disability justice delayed is disability justice denied)?[24]

Preferential Justice

Practically, a preferential justice for people with disability is neither too taxing on a community's resources nor extraordinarily unattainable. Taking a cue from the disability rights canon (human rights plus the sociology-identified models of disability affirmed in constitutional law and other legislative acts),[25] the unfortunately remarkable truth that people with disability are people first bears repeating. I remark "unfortunately" in order to keep in mind the harrowing experience and horrifying treatment of people with disability in such obscene and degrading ways to emphasize the unjust and abusive lack of welcome to the human community that has been the tragic story of scandalous injustice toward them. And I pronounce "remarkable" with the irony that is the truth about and justice for people with disability: they are people first, yes, and they are *imago Dei* thereby. It is for reasons of past and present injustice that today a preferential justice may stir the Christian churches to abide by the principles of the Universal Declaration of Human Rights (1948), the Civil Rights Act (1964), Americans with Disabilities Act (1990), and the Convention on the Rights of Persons with Disabilities (2006).[26] More importantly, for reasons concerning the *imago Dei*, discipleship champions justice. Before he went to trial, Jesus instructed us to extend support—to feed those who are hungry, give drink to those who thirst, clothe those with garments in tatters, visit those who are imprisoned, care for those who are sick, and welcome those who are strangers or aliens for whatever visible reasons they may appear different in kind from the main—yes, to extend support preferentially to such as these.[27]

The urgency of actualizing the preferential option with a preferential justice for people with disability and for the many others who have been denied the common good owed to them functions in the tradition of Catholic social teaching under the rubric of the universal destination of goods.[28] The function of this rubric holds an uncompromising sense of equity regarding everyone's share in the goods of Earth and of the work of human hands. The function summons a disposition toward relational dependence and material, personal, and spiritual care with and for one another. As noted in chapter 3, persons with disability are more likely than others to have been denied the natural law ground of the common good and its companion principle of the universal destination of goods that serve as the means for developing their basic functioning capabilities—to be, to love, to learn, to engage, and to thrive. The *Compendium of the Social Doctrine of the Church* is emphatic on the matter of access to those goods that are necessary for life in abundance and to thrive:

§172. Each person must have access to the level of well-being necessary for [her, zir, and] his full development. The right to the common use of goods is the 'first principle of the whole ethical and social order.'. . . It is first of all a *natural* right, inscribed in human nature and not merely a positive right connected with changing historical circumstances; moreover, it is an "inherent" right. It is innate in individual persons, in every person, and has *priority* with regard to any human intervention concerning goods, to any legal system concerning the same, to any economic or social system or method: "All other rights, whatever they are, including property rights and the right of free trade[,] must be subordinated to this norm [the universal destination of goods]; they must not hinder it, but must rather expedite its application. It must be considered a serious and urgent social obligation to refer these rights to their original purpose" (Paul VI, *Populorum Progressio* [1967], §22).

§175. The universal destination of goods requires a common effort to obtain for every person and for all peoples the conditions necessary for integral development, so that everyone can contribute to making a more human world, "in which each individual can give and receive, and in which the progress of some will no longer be an obstacle to the development of others, nor a pretext for their enslavement" (Congregation for the Doctrine of the Faith, *Libertatis Conscientia* [1987], §90).

§182. The principle of the universal destination of goods requires that the poor, the marginalized, and in all cases those whose living conditions interfere with their proper growth should be the focus of particular concern. To this end, the preferential option for the poor should be reaffirmed in all its force.[29]

When one member of the human community is hindered from or denied access to the goods necessary for the development and exercise of basic human functioning capabilities and to thrive, regardless of that member's proximity to the main, the whole community will suffer the poverty of the one, though not nearly as acutely nor without a means of escape. Those with ready access to the common good need not worry that their needs will go unmet; on the contrary, their security is assured in their privilege, in their personal and social support systems, and by means of their accumulated overabundance of wealth. The universal destination of goods requires that none be left wanting. This same requirement ensures as well that none fall beneath the threshold of capability development and that any who are at present below the threshold are to be raised without delay.[30] Therefore, for the sake of preferential justice, it behooves every community to ensure widely the distribution of goods necessary to life and to living well if for no other reason than to avoid the scandal of want among neighbors near and far (even the most hard-hearted may recoil in distress at the sight of abject poverty), but other reasons abound.

From the standpoint of the Christian tradition, nothing less than a share in God's provisions for human well-being and flourishing must be extended in decidedly preferential ways to persons with disability and others whose access to the common goods of shelter, family, friends, nutritious food and potable water, health care, education, employment, recreation, and worship is compromised. The means of moving forward in following God's gratuitous and overabundant donation of resources, including the gift of life to humankind and all of creation, ought to follow the logic of God's own justice as it can be discerned in the testaments of our traditions. "In the widest sense, it [justice, or *mišpāt*] means 'to put things right,' to intervene in a situation that is wrong, oppressive or out of control and to 'fix' it. . . . [M]*išpāt* is what needs to be done in a given situation if people and circumstances are to be restored to conformity with [God's righteousness]. . . . Justice is essentially relational and covenantal."[31] Thus, while a preferential justice for people with disability may appear to offer an unfair advantage, preferential justice does not override anyone's threshold of basic needs. Rather, justice in relational terms is distributed in the great or small geometric-proportioned measures necessary for the individual and the community to thrive.[32] Appearances can be deceiving. Aristotle and Thomas Aquinas instruct that distributive justice for each and all is established not with an arithmetic

calculation or equal distribution but instead with a geometric calculation resulting in a proportionate distribution of those goods that are
necessary for each to thrive.[33] The means to thrive (in exercise of the
basic human functioning capabilities) are the subject matter of the universal destination of goods ordained by God.

A relational/covenantal sense of justice for those who have been
impoverished is found in Deuteronomy (e.g., Dt 10, 14, 24), Psalms (e.g.,
Ps 107, 132, 146), and Isaiah (e.g., Is 35, 41, 61) as well as in the general
trajectory of the Good News transmitted in the Gospels, the Acts of the
Apostles, and Epistles wherein followers of the Way are instructed in
the work of right relationship and covenant steadfastness. Perhaps especially in the New Testament, liberation from the oppressions of poverty
expressed in the lack of material and social capital is acute: Jesus ush-
ers in the messianic age of the healing of social and personal ills alongside the conferral of blessings (cf. Mt 11:2–6 and Lk 7:18–23).[34] Surely,
the reversal of misfortunes experienced by persons with disability and
others who have been marginalized by the dominant and powerful with
the impositions of socially constructed hegemonies requires an intentional preferential option for relationship—as one of the most fundamental and universal of goods—if Christians are to be recognized as
Jesus's disciples today.

Intentionality and Inclusive Relationship

We know from Thomas Aquinas, his teachers, and his successors that an
intention is an object that we want to possess literally or figuratively as a
proximate end.[35] It is the thing about which we will for ourselves or for
others with whom we engage so as to enjoy the object/end intended,
in this case friendship. In other words, intentionality is deliberate:
relationships/friendships do not happen spontaneously; they must be
cultivated over time regardless of an immediate attraction, laissez-faire
disposition, or initial aversion toward another. If we—individuals and
communities—are to move toward a preferential justice for people with
disability and other persons who have been denied the development
and exercise of their capabilities, that movement must be intentional.

And given the insights gained from the projects of liberation theology, we must go to the places where those who have been maligned live and work and study and play and pray to learn what it means to "go and do likewise" as we would intend for ourselves.

First, discover ways to spend intentional time in the company of God. After all, if God is for us, God is waiting on us to be serious about the relationship that God wills to have with each of us as friend and prophet.[36] Sure, there is communal prayer and liturgical worship. And there may be meditational reading of the Scriptures. And then there is the heart-to-heart kind of conversation where a fugue plays the prayer of friendship intimacy beyond all telling.

Next, consider friendship and other relationship encounters. These relationships ought also to be cared for with an intentionality about time and presence concerning not their instrumental purpose but rather the integrity of the other as she/ze/he is, in the glory that comes with being *imago Dei* and the glory of God fully alive. Sure, there will be activities of work or play or study and meet-ups for a celebration or consolation, but there also needs to be mutuality, respect, and confidence.

Finally, in terms of reaching beyond one's own kin, intentionality is essential for disability justice and inclusive personal, communal, and ecclesial relationship. In these intentional relationships, those who have been absent through no fault of their own are welcomed, embraced, and called by name to be, to learn and become proficient, to participate, and to thrive. These intentional relationships may then begin to undo the failures of the past and the present to recognize the capabilities and desires of persons with disability and of others who have been marginalized; I suspect that many may very well yearn to care for and be with others in common cause, in friendship, in work, in play, and in worship.

✶ ✶ ✶

At this moment in time, we have a unique opportunity to get it right in regard to persons with disability as ourselves, in our families, among our friends, coworkers, communities, and churches. The universal destination of goods can be readily directed preferentially toward efforts of greater inclusion ideologically and structurally for people with disability and others who have been excluded similarly. Here is a hunger and a thirst for justice, not an expression of a pity-inspired charity or patronage but instead the kind to which Jesus points as marks of discipleship and of the blessed in this life and in the next.

Conclusion

Inclusion in Place of Neglect

The No Not Me's

    I am almost seventy and have suffered a long time from the recoil of the "no not me." When an autoimmune condition made walking difficult, a colleague had to REALLY push me to submit paperwork for a disabled parking permit because, well, "No. Not me." When trainers suggested I prep my cute little mixed breed for emotional support dog certification as well as therapy dog certification, I thought again hmm, "No. Not me." Reluctance to admit "weakness" and to show "difference" was a real issue in so many of my decisions, so was stigma. I did experience palpable, negative feedback when I decided to bravely share a diagnosis at work. Those reactions certainly reinforced my own concerns and fears about the "no not me."

    Oddly, experiences like surgery, the pandemic, and aging have made my disabilities more relatable to many. My prolonged use of a cane due to hip replacement surgery has made it easier to speak of mobility issues stemming from my autoimmune disease. The isolation, stress, and sadness most people experienced during the pandemic have opened discussions for many on anxiety and depression. And aging itself has leveled the playing field a bit, as friends now have similar issues with mobility, sight, hearing, and chronic or critical health conditions. I have listened long enough to learn that disabilities are an equal opportunity reality borne by so many.

    I am seeing progress. That is, I think, due in large part to the research and teaching work of individuals like Mary Jo, work that helps society remove the invisible stigmas and physical barriers so that when persons with disabilities overcome their own particular "no not me," they can thrive and open a path for others.

Valerie Turner

Most of this writing has pointed to raising the conscience and consciousness of the faithful in regard to people who do not have a place or who have limited access to the Good News in our churches and evangelization efforts. Of course, much more can and must be said and even more can and must be done. Sadly, attitudinal and financial challenges remain in the work of even nominal let alone full inclusion. Questions that concern institutionalizing the changes needed so that persons with disability and others who have been marginalized or otherwise oppressed are welcomed in all the places where people gather—to live, to learn, to work, to play, and to pray—are yet to be examined. These changes require engaging the preferential option in and a preferential justice for the practices of relationship and inclusive participation at all levels of discipleship, decision making, and design for what is right and just.

Neglect of anyone with desires to participate in the community is both unjust and a violation of the principles of solidarity and subsidiarity. Neglect of anyone with desires to access the common good means of developing the basic human functioning capabilities so as to thrive thereby is both unjust and a violation as well of the principles of natural law and the universal destination of goods. Neglect of anyone with desires to incarnate the glory of God fully alive is both an insult of the *imago Dei* and a sin against God, perhaps even the blasphemy against the Holy Spirit that cannot be forgiven because that neglect denigrates God in whose image all human beings are created (cf. Mk 3:22–30, Mt 12:31–32, and Lk 12:10).[1]

The subject of inclusion or neglect pertains immediately to working with or against God's own mission for humankind. In short, that mission is the human being fully alive. An agenda of inclusion engages at minimum acceptance of the radical dependence that is the quintessential nature of being human, inclusive of people with disability and others who have been marginalized for having deviated from the hegemonic norms of the dominant power. An agenda of inclusion embraces a preferential justice regarding the universal and common goods necessary to exercise the functional capabilities alongside of developing the gifts deemed desirable by the moral agent herself/zirself/himself, for each and for all. An agenda of inclusion affirms the kaleidoscopic fecundity of diversity in humankind and reckons that this diversity is the norm for humans and all other creatures. And an agenda of inclusion beckons nothing less than human flourishing arising from the anthropological mandates of radical dependence/each person's *imago Dei* dignity.

A preferential justice for those who have been neglected and are vulnerable as a result of race, gender, and disability demands more: nothing less than inclusion through solidarity, the promotion of peace, and the distribution of the common goods will do.

⁕ ⁕ ⁕

If we Christians want to know how well we have fared thus far in conceiving and implementing an inclusive community respectful of the *imago Dei* therein, then we need to look in and around our churches and in every gathering of the people. Given the likelihood that, liberally, as many as 25 percent of the world's people are living with disability, observers should notice people with disability comprising, conservatively, 10–15 percent of those present in our common places, our social gatherings, our liturgical spaces, and our councils, chanceries, classrooms, playgrounds, parsonages, and hierarchies—in our world. And where persons with disability are not present, observers must ask what physical, ideological, and attitudinal obstacles had been put in place long ago and remain in place today that prevent persons with disability from participating in the relationships of diversity and dependence that for humankind and a creation subject to seismic change reflect kaleidoscopic fecundity and God's own creative imaginary.

Once the obstacles to participation are identified they can then be dismantled, and hopefully the community marshals will exercise a preferential justice, despite the cost, to do so. Thus, commit to looking in and around again for obstacles missed the first time and then keep looking.

Further, do not presume to be able to recognize either the obvious or furtive obstacles to inclusion without the help of people with disability themselves. Their vision, like those of other marginalized peoples, is often more keen than that of the nondisabled in recognizing exclusionary glances, hints, and practices. As the history presented in the earlier chapters has shown, the perceptions of the nondisabled have been warped by hegemonic normativity/unexamined assumptions of superiority and the usurpation of a power that belongs to God alone but has oppressed many in ways at odds with God's designs for diversity.[2] On par with the observations of other peoples who have been impoverished by systems of oppression, the vision of people with disability is necessary to deconstruct exclusionary and neglectful practices against them. Their vision can also replace those exclusions with both life-affirming and diversity-affirming practices of inclusion.

Again, look in and around the spaces you occupy, for even with the voices of experience from persons with disability some of their perceptions too will have been influenced and distorted by the oppressions and assumptions of hegemonic normativity. By definition, hegemonic normativity turns into beliefs about where I or this one or that one or we fall or sit or occupy on the scale of normativity. The scale of hegemony will have been sufficiently internalized among both the privileged and the fecund diverse peoples on the margins—through no fault of their own. By their hegemony, members of the dominant able-bodied/able-minded community believe the lies and the blasphemies of their superiority. And by internalized oppressions, nondominant people come to believe the lies and the blasphemies about their being inferior, their having nothing to contribute to the main, or even about their own liberation and *imago Dei* dignity. Additionally tragic, this self-oppression confirms the stereotypes of the "other" that others have assigned a similar disvalue from the main.[3] This work of liberation (like feminist, Black, Hispanic/Latinx, LGBTQ, and Indigenous peoples' liberation) requires the support of a village, a community, and the Catholic Church.

Further, if we want to guard against presuming wrongly that persons with disability are inferior to the nondisabled or that the nondisabled know what is "patronizingly" best for them, then the nondisabled will need to ensure that, as a rule, they hold steadfast to being accountable to persons with disability in their midst. Accountability, properly exercised, follows the norms of solidarity in friendship and subsidiarity in decision making by advocating with and for people while remaining attentive to the diversities of disability and the diversities of the needs that each person—those with and those without disability—will have now and again. Accountability to any people who have been oppressed requires their presence at the tables where power is exercised. In disability justice, accountability requires that people with disability participate fully in their futures and in the future of our inclusive churches. And accountability protects persons with disability against paternalism and the impositions of presumed norms as it liberates persons with disability to be themselves in all their glory as the *imago Dei* and as participants in the work of bringing the Good News of the fullness of life through Christ to all creation.

A Theology-Inspired Practical Takeaway for Inclusion

The premises of a theological anthropology of radical relational dependence continue. The insights of Catholic social teaching inform. And the sins against the *imago Dei* in the Person of Jesus of Nazareth and in the innumerable peoples marginalized and oppressed across the millennia require reckoning, repairing, and reconciling if we, the People of God, the Church, are to be disciples of the Risen Disabled God.

Inclusion must be the modus operandi of an agenda contra neglect:

In the Incarnation, in the Divine self-emptying *kenosis*, God bends over backwards—so in love for and merciful toward humankind is God for us—so as to become human. No minimum of effort or limit can be found in that *kenosis*. In fact, even to death does Jesus bend—nearly eviscerated, possibly raped or impaled,[4] and rather completely and shamefully stigmatized—in command and loving all the way to crucifixion and resurrected life. *Kenosis*, folly to the Greeks and blasphemy to the Jews, is shameful and illustrative of the lengths to which God bends for us. God is simply not capable of anything but the most and the best and more, including the self-emptying into human matter and spirit, that God can, would, did and does do. Admittedly, we fail to so bend time and again: we begrudge equal employment opportunities, equal access to education and healthcare, equal welcome to our places of gathering and worship, and we fail thereby solidarity and the preferential option, we fail to do what God wills. Nevertheless, we each are called to persevere in aligning our wills to God's will and thus as well to God's will for others we do not yet know. . . .

What practical take-away can be used to check accountability to and solidarity with people so as to live a preferential option for those who are marginalized, to do what is right and just and best? As a start, interrogate the past with a view to interrogate the present.

1) Retrieve the dangerous memories and scandals of the past. Listen to the voices of wisdom with those who have been marginalized on the basis of their "deviance" from the dominant norms and follow their lead for change. . . .

2) Dismantle what those who have been marginalized identify as oppressive and repressive structures and attitudes, inclusive of veiled microaggressions that lead to internalized inferiority and self-hate among minoritized people while . . . empower[ing] and embolden[ing] the dominant to dominate again. . . .

3) Internalize a hermeneutic of solidarity with and a preferential option for those who are marginalized. . . .

4) Then, look in and around common spaces—churches, schools, commercial and recreational venues, and government, in every gathering of the people—to note who is there and who is absent. . . . Where the gatherings are monochrome and/or mono-abled, there exclusionary practices of physical and/or attitudinal obstacles persist.

5) Repeat: listen and speak again with [one another and in] equal regard, then together assess results of the dismantling of oppression, brainstorm next steps with additional expertise, and follow the lead of wisdom for solidarity and the preferential option to make change.[5]

"God's mission has always taken place in the midst of Empire."[6] As past practice is exposed and rejected for an agenda contrary to God's purposes, something new must fill the spaces once occupied by failure and sin against the *imago Dei*. Then the dangerous memory of Jesus's passion and the suffering deaths of an untold multitude of others will be redeemed not by neglect or death but instead by preferential justice, inclusive love, and forgiveness of sin. This future will interrupt the logic of Empire and its commitments to dominate those deemed undesirable or unworthy of the common good. Again, as these insights come now from people on the peripheries of ecclesial, political, and social spheres of influence, from those who witness the Good News of liberation that God is for us in our fecund asymmetry: in this diversity the relevance of our churches depends—and radically so—on our partnerships, solidarity, and preferential justice with all who have been and continue to be excluded from the main.

The global reality that is people with disability, real flesh-and-blood neighbors, remains in need of attention by all the powers amassed against the welcome to which all people ought to enjoy except for the ignorance and greed of those who hold the power of an empire that foolishly champions hegemony where diversity prevails. If God is for us and if we are attentive to the full range of diversity present within humankind, then how can any one of us not challenge the folly of hegemony? I suggest at minimum—where God goes to the maximum in identifying with humankind by kenosis to a stigmatizing death—that we, who call ourselves disciples of the Crucified God, make inclusion the norm and measure of our discipleship.

— NOTES —

Introduction

1. Among others, see Shelley Tremain, "Foucault, Governmentality, and Critical Disability Theory Today: A Genealogy of the Archive," in *Foucault and the Government of Disability*, ed. Shelley Tremain, 9–26 (Ann Arbor: University of Michigan Press, 2015); and Dan Goodley, "Dis/entangling Critical Disability Studies," *Disability & Society* 28.5 (2013): 631–44.
2. The Jewish Federation, Committee on Inclusion and Disabilities, "Mission," 2012, http://jewishsac.org/inclusionanddisabilities/.
3. Rooshey Hasnain, Laura Cohon Shaikh, and Hasan Shanawani, *Disability and the Muslim Perspective: An Introduction for Rehabilitation and Health Care Providers* (Buffalo, NY: State University of New York, 2008), 27.
4. In Jewish, Christian, and Muslim usage following the biblical account (Genesis 1:26–27), the *imago Dei* points to a theo-anthropological claim that human beings are created in the image and likeness of God.
5. Miguel J. Romero and Mary Jo Iozzio, eds., "Engaging Disability," special issue, *Journal of Moral Theology* 2, SI 2 (Fall 2017).
6. Susan Wendell, "Toward a Feminist Theory of Disability," *Hypatia* 4.2 (1989): 104–24.
7. See Mary Jo Iozzio, "Justice Is a Virtue Both in and out of Healthcare," *Irish Theological Quarterly* 63.2 (1998): 151–66.
8. Among others, see Adrienne Asch, "Prenatal Diagnosis and Selective Abortion: A Challenge to Practice and Policy," *American Journal of Public Health* 89 (1999): 1649–1657. Related, consider the expectation to abort on genetic grounds of the 2018–19 debates on the US Supreme Court Case *Roe v. Wade* (1973), No. 70-18.

Chapter 1. Disability Basics

1. Nina Farahanchi, "It's Time to Talk about the World's Largest Minority," TEDxYouth@AnnArbor, TEDx Talks, June 25, 2018, https://www.youtube .com/watch?v=-PbG3f98MpM.
2. WHO, *International Classification of Functioning, Disability and Health* (Geneva: World Health Organization, 2001); WHO, *International Classification of Functioning, Disability and Health: Children & Youth Version* (Geneva: World Health Organization, 2007).
3. I am here combining the terms of federal regulations regarding the Americans with Disabilities Act and the specific disabilities covered for children under the Individuals with Disabilities Education Act (reauthorized in 2004 and amended in the Every Student Succeeds Act of 2015). See ADA, "Law/Regulations," United States Department of Justice, Civil Rights Division, n.d., https://www.ada.gov/2010_regs.htm; and US Department of Education, Individuals with Disabilities Education Act, "About IDEA," n.d., https://sites.ed.gov/idea/.
4. Among others, see Lori Golden, "Diversity Leaders: 6 Things NEVER to Say about Disabilities," DiversityInc, September 10, 2018, https:// www.diversityinc.com/diversity-leaders-6-things-never-to-say-about -disabilities; Kristin Duquette and Mary Hums, "10 Crucial Ways We Can Make Society More Inclusive for People with Disabilities," Huffington Post, August 25, 2016, https://www.huffingtonpost.com/kristin -duquette/10-crucial-ways-we-can-make-society-more-inclusive-for -people-with-disabilities_b_8027718.html; and PWDA, "Resources: Language Guide," People with Disability Australia, 2018, https://pwd.org .au/resources/language-guide/.
5. United Spinal Association, *Disability Etiquette: Tips on Interacting with People with Disabilities* (Kew Gardens, NY: United Spinal Association, 2015), http://www.unitedspinal.org/pdf/DisabilityEtiquette.pdf.
6. Among others, see Colin Barnes, Geoffrey Mercer, and Tom Shakespeare, "The Social Model of Disability," in *Sociology: Introductory Readings*, ed. Anthony Giddens and Philip W. Sutton, 161–66 (Cambridge, UK: Polity, 2010); Simona D'Alessio, *Inclusive Education in Italy: A Critical Analysis of the Policy of 'Integrazione Scolastica'* (Rotterdam, Netherlands: Sense Publishers, 2011); and Michael Oliver, "A New Model of the Social Work Role in Relation to Disability," in *The Handicapped Person: A New Perspective for Social Workers*, ed. Jo Campling, 19–32 (London: Radar, 1981).
7. WHO, "Disabilities," Health Topics, 2019, https://www.who.int/topics /disabilities/en/.

8. See WHO, *Towards a Common Language for Functioning, Disability and Health: ICF* (Geneva: World Health Organization, 2002), 8–14.

9. Union of Physically Impaired Against Segregation, *Fundamental Principles of Disability*, November 22, 1975, https://disability-studies.leeds.ac.uk/wp-content/uploads/sites/40/library/UPIAS-fundamental-principles.pdf.

10. See Wolf Wolfensberger, *The Principles of Normalization* (Toronto: National Institute on Mental Retardation, 1972); and Wolf Wolfensberger, *The Origin and Nature of Our Institutional Models* (Syracuse, NY: Human Policy, 1974).

11. With exceptions to quoted material, my choice to use the singular "disability" follows the lead of people with disability, who recognize the potentially problematic overgeneralization suggestive of the plural "disabilities." See PWDA, "Resources: Language Guide."

12. LEAD Center and Job Accommodation Network, *Effective Communication: Disability Awareness & Etiquette Guide* (Washington, DC: National Disability Institute, 2016), http://www.leadcenter.org/system/files/resource/downloadable_version/CIL-LEAD-JAN-Effective-Communication-Guide-WIOA.pdf.

13. WHO and World Bank, *World Report on Disability* (Geneva: World Health Organization, 2011), 8.

14. This history is decidedly inadequate. However, for readers unfamiliar with the trajectories of experiences for persons with disability, I offer here but a glimpse of such experiences in the aggregate. Individuals have fared far better and far worse than what follows. My purpose here is solely introductory. The history is complex and was uncovered often with a focus on who is missing from many narratives and who is referred to in the prescripts of laws and customary mores. In addition to the references that follow in the text, see Roy Hanes, Ivan Brown, and Nancy E. Hansen, *The Routledge History of Disability* (New York: Routledge, 2017); Michael Rembis, Catherine J. Kudlick, and Kim E. Nielsen, eds., *The Oxford Handbook of Disability History* (New York: Oxford University Press, 2018); and Bill Hughes, *A Historical Sociology of Disability: Human Validity and Invalidity from Antiquity to Early Modernity* (New York: Routledge, 2020).

15. In addition to these three models, other precisions have been offered with the tragedy/charity, expert/professional, rehabilitation, economic, and rights-based customer-empowering models. See Tom Shakespeare, "Cultural Representation of Disabled People: Dustbins for Disavowal?," *Disability & Society* 9.3 (1994): 283–99; Deborah Marks, "Models of Disability," *Disability and Rehabilitation* 19.3 (1997): 85–91; A. Llewellyn

and K. Hogan, "The Use and Abuse of Models of Disability," *Disability &*
Society 15.1 (2000): 157–65; Carmelo Masala and Donatella Rita Petretto,
"Models of Disability," in *International Encyclopedia of Rehabilitation*,
ed. J. H. Stone and M. Blouin (Buffalo, NY: Center for International Rehabilitation Research Information and Exchange, 2010); and Mike Oliver,
"The Social Model of Disability: Thirty Years On," *Disability & Society*
28.7 (2013): 1024–26.

16. See Wolf Wolfensberger, *A Brief Overview of Social Role Valorization: A*
High-Order Concept for Addressing the Plight of Societally Devalued People
and for Structuring Human Services (Plantagenet, Ontario; Valor, 2013),
originally published by the Training Institute for Human Service Planning,
Syracuse, NY, 1998, 2004.

17. See Erving Goffman, *Stigma: Notes on the Management of Spoiled Identity*
(New York: Simon & Schuster, 1963).

18. On the ramifications of a culture of silence, see Paulo Freire, "The Adult
Literacy Process as Cultural Action for Freedom" and "Cultural Action and
Conscientization," *Harvard Educational Review* 68.4 (1998): 480–98, 499–
521, originally published in *Harvard Educational Review* 40.2–3 (1970):
205–25, 452–77.

19. Paulo Freire, Michel Foucault, Iris Marion Young, and others have written
extensively on power, cultural imperialism, and marginalization. Freire's
thought is instructive: "In the culture of silence the masses are 'mute,' that
is, they are prohibited from creatively taking part in the transformations of
their society and therefore prohibited from being. Even if they can occa-
sionally read and write because they were 'taught' in humanitarian—but
not humanist—literacy campaigns, they are nevertheless alienated from
the power responsible for their silence." Freire, "The Adult Literacy Process," 486.

20. See Colin Barnes, "A Legacy of Oppression: A History of Disability in
Western Culture," in *Disability Studies: Past, Present, and Future*, ed.
C. Barnes and Mike Oliver, 3–24 (Leeds, UK: The Disability Press, 1997);
Tom Shakespeare, "Cultural Representation of Disabled People: Dustbins
for Disavowal?," *Disability & Society* 9.3 (1994): 283–99; Henri-Jacques
Stiker, *A History of Disability*, trans. William Sayers (Ann Arbor: Univer-
sity of Michigan Press, 2000); and Eli Clare, *Brilliant Imperfection: Grap-*
pling with Cure (Durham, NC: Duke University Press, 2017).

21. Although the web has a host of sites started and managed by people with
disability, one example of a history project led by people with disability
is "Disability History Timeline," Disability Social History Project, 2014,
https://disabilityhistory.org/moments-in-disability-history/. See also Peter

Catapano and Rosemarie Garland-Thomson, *About Us: Essays from the Disability Series of the New York Times* (New York: Liveright Publishing, 2019).

22. See Masala and Petretto, "Models of Disability."
23. See Wolfensberger, *A Brief Overview of Social Role Valorization.*
24. See Goffman, *Stigma.*
25. See Richard Slayton French, *From Homer to Helen Keller: A Social and Educational Study of the Blind* (New York: American Foundation for the Blind, 1932).
26. Robert Garland, *The Eye of the Beholder: Deformity and Disability in the Graeco-Roman World* (Lyndhurst, NJ: Barnes & Noble/Bristol Classical Paperbacks, [1995] 2010).
27. See Aristotle, *Sense and Sensibilia* 1 (437a16), trans. J. I. Beare (Boston: Classics MIT; The Internet Classics Archive, Daniel C. Stevenson, Web Atomics, 1994–2009), http://classics.mit.edu/Aristotle/sense.html; Aristotle, *Politics*, Book VII, 16 (1335b20), trans. Benjamin Jowett (Boston: Classics MIT; The Internet Classics Archive, Daniel C. Stevenson, Web Atomics, 1994–2009), http://classics.mit.edu/Aristotle/politics.html; and Seneca the Elder, *Controversiae*, IV, especially "Mendici Debilitati," trans. W. Winderbottom (Cambridge, MA: Harvard University Press, 1974).
28. William Stearns Davis, *A Day in Old Athens* (Ann Arbor: University of Michigan Library, [1910] 2009), 57. See also Harold Bennett, "The Exposure of Infants in Ancient Rome," *Classical Journal* 18 (1923): 341–51.
29. Among others, see Matthew Parry, *From Monsters to Patients: A History of Disability* (PhD diss., Arizona State University, 2013); and John Boswell, *The Kindness of Strangers: The Abandonment of Children in Western Europe from Late Antiquity to the Renaissance* (New York: Pantheon Books, 1988).
30. Among others, see Hector Avalos, Sarah J. Melcher, and Jeremy Schipper, eds., *This Abled Body: Rethinking Disabilities in Biblical Studies* (Atlanta: Society of Biblical Literature, 2007); Saul M. Olyan, *Disability in the Hebrew Bible: Interpreting Mental and Physical Differences* (New York: Cambridge University Press, 2008); and Louise J. Lawrence, *Sense and Stigma in the Gospels: Depictions of Sensory-Disabled Characters* (New York: Oxford University Press, 2013).
31. See Job chaps. 4–31. Of course, the multiple discourses within the book of Job argue the purpose(s) of the afflictions that Job experiences with dramatic affect and ultimately reject conclusions that his affliction is punishment for purported wrongdoing. Alternately, the dialogues between Job and his friends and Job with God suggest something more akin to "the sublimity of the cosmos." See Rebecca Raphael, "Things Too Wonderful:

A Disabled Reading of Job," *Perspectives in Religious Studies* 31.4 (2004): 399–424. That sublime reality, I suggest, points directly to my and others' proposal for the kaleidoscopic diversity of creation.

32. See Sharon Farmer, "The Beggar's Body: Intersections of Gender and Social Status," and Catherine Peyroux, "The Leper's Kiss," in *Monks & Nuns, Saints & Outcasts*, ed. Sharon Farmer and Barbara H. Rosenwein, 153–71 and 172–88 (Ithaca, NY: Cornell University Press, 2000).

33. Zita Turi, "Border Liners: The Ship of Fools Tradition in Sixteenth Century England," *Trans—Revue de littérature générale et comparée* 10 (2010), https://doi.org/10.4000/trans.421.

34. See the discussion of "positive eugenics" in Albert Jonsen, *The Birth of Bioethics* (New York: Oxford University Press, 1998), 169–72. On the biological basis of racial discrimination, see, for example, Harriet A. Washington, *Medical Apartheid: The Dark History of Medical Experimentation on Black Americans from Colonial Times to the Present* (New York: Doubleday, 2006).

35. See Adam Cohen, *Imbeciles: The Supreme Court, American Eugenics, and the Sterilization of Carrie Buck* (New York: Penguin Books, 2016); and Molly McCully Brown, *The Virginia State Colony for Epileptics and Feebleminded* (New York: Persea Books, 2017).

36. Among others, see Alicia Ouellette, *Bioethics and Disability: Toward a Disability-Conscious Bioethics* (New York: Cambridge University Press, 2011); Nirmala Erevelles, *Disability and Difference in Global Contexts: Enabling a Transformative Body Politic* (New York: Palgrave Macmillan, 2011); and Allison Kafer, *Feminist, Queer, Crip* (Bloomington: Indiana University Press, 2013).

37. See Mary Jo Iozzio, "Genetic Anomaly or Genetic Diversity: Thinking in the Key of Disability," *Theological Studies* 66.3 (2005): 862–81; and Mary Jo Iozzio, "Thinking about Disabilities with Justice, Liberation, and Mercy," *Horizons* 36.1 (2009): 32–49.

38. Elizabeth Johnson, *She Who Is: The Mystery of God in Feminist Theological Discourse* (New York: Crossroad Publishing, 1996), 219.

39. See Margaret Farley, "A Feminist Version of Respect for Persons," *Journal of Feminist Studies in Religion* 9.1–2 (1983): 183–98.

40. See Martha Nussbaum, "Human Capabilities, Female Human Beings," in *Women, Culture, and Development: A Study of Human Capabilities*, ed. Martha Nussbaum and Jonathan Glover, 61–104 (Oxford, UK: Clarendon, 1995).

41. See John Zizioulas, "Communion and Otherness," *St. Vladimir's Theological Quarterly* 38.4 (1994): 347–61; and Hans Reinders, *Receiving the Gift of Friendship: Profound Disability, Theological Anthropology, and Ethics* (Grand Rapids, MI: William B. Eerdmans, 2008).

42. See Alasdair MacIntyre, "Why the Enlightenment Project of Justifying Morality Had to Fail," in *After Virtue*, 51–61 (Notre Dame, IN: University of Notre Dame Press, 1984).
43. See Brian Clark, *Whose Life Is It Anyway?* (1972), original television production for the BBC acted on New York's Broadway in 1978. Set in a hospital room, the action revolves around a sculptor by profession who was paralyzed from the neck down (quadriplegia) in a car accident and argues, quite persuasively, to be allowed to die. Clark presented arguments both in favor of and opposing euthanasia and to what extent government should be allowed to interfere in a "rational person's" decision to die.
44. See Nancy Mairs, *A Dynamic God: Living an Unconventional Catholic Faith* (Boston: Beacon, 2007); and Philip M. Ferguson, Alan Gartner, and Dorothy K. Lipsky, "The Experience of Disability in Families: A Synthesis of Research and Parent Narratives," in *Prenatal Testing and Disability Rights*, ed. Erik Parens and Adrienne Asch, 72–92 (Washington, DC: Georgetown University Press, 2000).
45. See BBC News, "Happiness and Disability," Interview with Tom Shakespeare, *Sunday Magazine* (June 1, 2014), https://www.bbc.com/news/magazine -27554754; and Tom Shakespeare, "A Life Worth Living," in *Disability: The Basics* (New York, Routledge, 2018), 45–67.
46. Hence, at 1.7 percent, the 2017 total fertility rate in the United States, at a record low of 60.3 births per 1,000 women of childbearing age, is below population replacement needs. Bradley E. Hamilton, Joyce A. Martin, Michelle J. K. Osterman, Anne K. Driscoll, and Lauren M. Rossen, "Births: Provisional Data for 2017," *Vital Statistics Rapid Release*, no. 4 (Hyattsville, MD: National Center for Health Statistics, 2018), https://www.cdc .gov/nchs/data/vsrr/report004.pdf. This downward trend continues, with data of the first quarter of 2019 indicating a birth rate of 58.8 per 1,000 women of childbearing age. National Center for Health Statistics, "General Fertility Rates," 2017—Quarter 2, 2019, https://www.cdc.gov/nchs/nvss /vsrr/natality-dashboard.htm.
47. Olyan, *Disability in the Hebrew Bible*, 5–6.
48. See *Oxford English Dictionary* (1989), s.v. "stigma." See also the now classic exploration of stigma by Erving Goffman, *Stigma*; Erving Goffman, "Control by Word Power, II: The Structure of Remedial Interchanges," in *Life Sentences: Aspects of the Social Role of Language*, ed. Rom Harre, 66–74 (New York: Wiley, 1976); U.S. Department of Health and Human Services, *Mental Health: A Report of the Surgeon General* (Washington, DC, 1999); and Janet Nelson, "Bioethics and the Marginalization of Mental Illness," *Journal of the Society of Christian Ethics* 23.2 (2003): 179–97.

49. See Wolf Wolfensberger, "A Brief Overview of Social Role Valorization," *Mental Retardation* 38 (2000): 105–24.

50. Michel Foucault, "The Subject and Power," in *Power*, trans. by Robert Hurley et al. (New York: New Press, 1994), 326.

51. See Bruce G. Link and Jo C. Phelan, "Conceptualizing Stigma," *Annual Review of Sociology* 27 (2001): 367.

52. See Richard E. Whitaker, comp., *The Eerdmans Analytical Concordance to the Revised Standard Version of the Bible* (Grand Rapids, MI: Wm. B. Eerdmans, 1988).

53. See Lennard J. Davis, *Enforcing Normalcy: Disability, Deafness and the Body* (New York: Verso, 1995); Lennard J. Davis, *Bending Over Backwards: Essays on Disability and the Body* (New York: New York University Press, 2002); Herbert C. Covey, *Social Perceptions of People with Disabilities* (Springfield, IL: Charles C. Thomas, 1998); and Rosemarie Garland-Thomson, *Extraordinary Bodies* (New York: Columbia University Press, 1997).

54. Although other words may have been used to identify persons with disabilities, I developed this short list of what I think may be the most common evidence of attention to disability.

55. Similar to the ways that the Priestly literature and Deuteronomy restrict women's participation in cultic acts, so were people with disability (the blind, the lame, those with some blemish, skin disease, physical defect, crushed testicles or eunuch, and other) deemed unfit and thereby disqualified from altar service at communal ritual activities. See Sarah J. Melcher, "Blemish and Perfection in the Priestly Literature and Deuteronomy," *Journal of Religion, Disability & Health* 16.1 (2012): 1–15. As a counterpoint, Melcher argues that "Isaiah 56:1–8 seeks to change exclusion to inclusion for the foreigner and the eunuch, who has previously been regarded as having a disqualifying defect" (10). Olyan argues similarly on the seemingly contradictory futures for persons with disability. See Olyan, "Disability in the Prophetic Utopian Vision," in *Disability in the Hebrew Bible*, 78–92.

56. Olyan, *Disability in the Hebrew Bible*, 26; on the Dead Sea Scrolls, see 101–18.

57. See Covey, *Social Perceptions of People with Disabilities*, 26–30.

Chapter 2. Contributions from the United Nations and the World Health Organization

1. See Mary Jo Iozzio, "Building Coalitions with NGOs: Religion Scholars and Disability Justice Activism," *Religions* 9.1 (2018): 1–18. Both organizations work consultatively with service professionals and academics in

many other disciplines, from health care to the humanities and other social and empirical sciences.

2. WHO, "Disability and Health," Fact Sheets (Geneva: World Health Organization, 2018), http://www.who.int/en/news-room/fact-sheets/detail/disability-and-health.

3. See Peiyun She and David C. Stapleton, *A Review of Disability Data for the Institutional Population* (Washington, DC: Cornell University Institute for Policy Research, 2006), http://digitalcommons.ilr.cornell.edu/cgi/viewcontent.cgi?article=1205&context=edicollect.

4. The 2010 US census finds 20 percent of noninstitutionalized people (57 million of 300 million). See US Census Bureau, "Nearly 1 in 5 Have a Disability in the US," July 25, 2012, https://www.census.gov/newsroom/releases/archives/miscellaneous/cb12-134.html. Census figures for 2017 indicate a reduction in the number of noninstitutionalized people with disability in the United States to 13.3 percent of 323 million. See Danielle Taylor, *Disability Statistics from the US Census Bureau 2017/2018* (Washington, DC: US Department of Commerce, February 13, 2018), https://disabilitycompendium.org/sites/default/files/user-uploads/Events/Comp2017Presentations/danielle-taylor-2.13.18.pdf.

5. UN, "Preamble," Charter of the United Nations, June 16, 1945, http://www.un.org/en/sections/un-charter/preamble/index.html.

6. UN, Universal Declaration of Human Rights, December 10, 1948, http://www.un.org/en/universal-declaration-human-rights/index.html.

7. UN, "World Programme of Action Concerning Disabled Persons," 1982, https://www.un.org/development/desa/disabilities/resources/world-programme-of-action-concerning-disabled-persons.html.

8. UN, "Convention on the Rights of Persons with Disabilities," December 13, 2006, https://www.un.org/development/desa/disabilities/convention-on-the-rights-of-persons-with-disabilities.html#Fulltext. The United States signed the convention on July 30, 2009. Frustrating to many, however, and despite President Barack Obama's signature, the United States has not yet ratified its consent to be bound by the convention.

9. UN, "Preamble," Convention on the Rights of Persons with Disabilities, December 13, 2006, https://www.un.org/development/desa/disabilities/convention-on-the-rights-of-persons-with-disabilities/preamble.html.

10. UNDESA, "Our Mandates," 2006, https://www.un.org/development/desa/disabilities/about-us/our-mandates.html.

11. Centers for Disease Control and Prevention, "Washington Group on Disability Statistics," 2016, http://www.cdc.gov/nchs/washington_group.htm. The Washington Group on Disability Statistics (http://www.washingtongroup

-disability.com/), established by the UN Statistical Commission, provides tools for assessing disability across the globe.

12. UNDESA, "Disability," n.d., https://www.un.org/development/desa/dis abilities/.

13. UN, "News on Millennium Development Goals," n.d., http://www.un.org /millenniumgoals/.

14. UN, "Sustainable Development," n.d., https://sustainabledevelopment.un .org.

15. UNDESA, "In Focus," n.d., https://www.un.org/development/desa/dis abilities/in-focus.html.

16. UNDESA, *UN Flagship Report on Disability and Sustainable Development Goals*, 2018, https://www.un.org/development/desa/disabilities /publication-disability-sdgs.html.

17. See Arlene S. Kanter, "Let's Try Again: Why the United States Should Ratify the United Nations Conventions on the Rights of People with Disabilities," *Touro Law Review* 35.1 (2019): 301–43.

18. UN, "Resolution Adopted by the General Assembly," Fifty-Eighth Session, Agenda item 106 (December 22, 2003), http://www.un.org/disabilities /default.asp?id=67.

19. UN, "General Assembly High-Level Meeting on Disability and Development, 23 September 2013," https://www.un.org/en/desa/high-level -meeting-disabilities-and-development-23-september-2013.

20. UN, "#Envision2030: 17 Goals to Transform the World for Persons with Disabilities," n.d., https://www.un.org/development/desa/disabilities/envision 2030.html.

21. UNDESA, *Realization of the Sustainable Development Goals*, 1 (April 3, 2019), https://www.un.org/development/desa/dspd/2019/04/un-disability -and-development-report-realizing-the-sdgs-by-for-and-with-persons -with-disabilities/.

22. See Sophie Mitra, Aleksandra Posarac, and Brandon Vick, *Disability and Poverty in Developing Countries: A Snapshot from the World Health Survey*, World Bank Social Protection and Labor Unit, 2011, http:// siteresources.worldbank.org/SOCIALPROTECTION/Resources/SP -Discussion-papers/Disability-DP/1109.pdf.

23. UN, *Disability and the Millennium Development Goals: A Review of the MDG Process and Strategies for Inclusion of Disability Issues in Millennium Development Goal Efforts* (New York: United Nations, 2011), 8, 12–13, https://www.un.org/disabilities/documents/review_of_disability_and_the _mdgs.pdf.

24. See Claudia Bell, "Disability in the Context of Armed Conflict Situations," International Conference: Disasters Are Always Inclusive! Persons with

Disabilities in Humanitarian Emergency Situations, November 7–8, 2007, Bonn, Germany, http://www.bezev.de/fileadmin/Neuer_Ordner/Literatur /Bibliothek/Tagungsdokumentationen/Humanitaere_Hilfe/hi_dok _disability_and_conflict_07-endv.pdf; Mary Jo Iozzio, "The Other Casualties of War: Soldiers and Civilians with Disabilities, Compromised Care Systems, and Responsive Ethical Reasoning," and Iozzio, "Ethical Implications of War-Borne Disabling Casualties," *Journal of Religion, Disability & Health* 12.3 (2003): 207–13 and 287–302 (this issue of the journal is dedicated to the subject "The Other Casualties of War").

25. Shantha Rau Barriga, "Dispatches: Invisible Victims of the Syrian Conflict—People with Disabilities," Human Rights Watch, September 19, 2013, http://www.hrw.org/news/2013/09/19/dispatches-invisible-victims -syrian-conflict-people-disabilities.

26. See Handicap International, "Syria: One Million Injured, a Mutilated Future," 2014, http://handicap-international.ca/en/syria-one-million-injured-a -mutilated-future. See also Sarah Gillam, "Hidden Victims: New Research on Older, Disabled, and Injured Syrian Refugees," HelpAge International, September 4, 2014, http://www.helpage.org/newsroom/latest -news/hidden-victims-new-research-on-older-disabled-and-injured -syrian-refugees/.

27. Global Disability Summit 2018, "Charter for Change," https://assets .publishing.service.gov.uk/government/uploads/system/uploads /attachment_data/file/721701/GDS_Charter_for_Change.pdf.

28. See World Bank Group, "World Bank Group Commitments on Disability Inclusive Development," 2018, http://www.worldbank.org/en/topic /socialdevelopment/brief/world-bank-group-commitments-on-disability -inclusion-development.

29. World Bank Group, *Disability Inclusion and Accountability Framework* (Washington, DC: International Bank for Reconstruction and Development, 2018), iv, http://documents.worldbank.org/curated/en/437451528 442789278/pdf/126977-WP-PUBLIC-DisabilityInclusionAccountability digital.pdf.

30. See Tomoko Akami, "A Quest to Be Global: The League of Nations Health Organization and the Inter-Colonial Regional Governing Agendas of the Far Eastern Association of Tropical Medicine 1910–25," *International History Review* 38.1 (2016): 1–23; N. Howard Jones, "Origins of International Health Work," *British Medical Journal* 1.4661 (1950): 1032–37; and Nova et Vetera, "The International Health Organization of the League of Nations," *British Medical Journal* 1.3302 (1924): 672–75.

31. Paul Weindling, "The League of Nations Health Organization and the Rise of Latin American Participation, 1920–40," *História, Ciências,*

Saúde-Manguinhos 13.3 (2006), http://www.scielo.br/scielo.php?pid=S0104 -59702006000300002&script=sci_arttext&tlng=en.

32. WHO, "Constitution of the World Health Organization," in *Basic Documents* (Geneva: World Health Organization, 2014), 1–2, http://apps.who .int/gb/bd/PDF/bd48/basic-documents-48th-edition-en.pdf#page=1.

33. UN, Office of the High Commissioner on Human Rights, "International Covenant on Economic, Social and Cultural Rights," Article 12 (December 16, 1966, entry into force January 3, 1976), http://www.ohchr.org/EN /ProfessionalInterest/Pages/CESCR.aspx.

34. See WHO, *International Classification of Functioning, Disability and Health* (Geneva: World Health Organization, 2001); WHO, *International Classification of Functioning, Disability and Health: Children & Youth Version* (Geneva: World Health Organization, 2007); WHO and World Bank, *World Report on Disability* (Geneva: World Health Organization, 2011); and WHO, *WHO Global Disability Action Plan 2014–2021: Better Health for All People with Disability* (Geneva: World Health Organization, 2015).

35. See Amartya Sen, *Collective Choice and Social Welfare: An Expanded Edition* (Cambridge, MA: Harvard University Press, 2017).

36. See Michael Oliver, *The Politics of Disablement* (London: Macmillan, 1990); and Susan Wendell, *The Rejected Body* (New York: Routledge, 1996).

37. See Martha Nussbaum, *Frontiers of Justice: Disability, Nationality, and Species Membership* (Cambridge, MA: Harvard University Press, 2006); Amartya Sen, "Capability and Well-Being," in *The Quality of Life*, ed. Martha Nussbaum and Amartya Sen, 30–53 (Oxford, UK: Clarendon, 1993).

38. See Amartya Sen, *The Idea of Justice* (Cambridge, MA: Harvard University Press, 2009); and Martha C. Nussbaum, *Frontiers of Justice: Disability, Nationality, Species Membership* (Cambridge, MA: Harvard University Press, 2007).

39. See Mary Jo Iozzio, "Norms Matter: A Hermeneutic of Disability/a Theological Anthropology of Radical Dependence," *ET-Studies* 4.1 (2013): 89–106.

40. See Deborah Creamer, "Theological Accessibility: The Contribution of Disability," *Disability Studies Quarterly* 26.4 (2006), http://dsq-sds.org/article /view/812/987; and Scot Danforth, "Liberation Theology of Disability and the Option for the Poor," *Disability Studies Quarterly* 25.3 (2005), http:// dsq-sds.org/article/view/572/749.

41. Adapted from Martha Nussbaum, "Human Capabilities, Female Human Beings," in *Women, Culture, and Development: A Study of Human Capabilities*, ed. Martha Nussbaum and Jonathan Glover, 83–85 (Oxford: Clarendon Press, 1995).

42. See WHO and World Bank, *World Report on Disability*, 7–8.
43. WHO and World Bank, 262.
44. Among others, see World Bank, "Understanding Poverty," World Bank Group, 2018, https://www.worldbank.org/en/topic/disability; Kristen Bialik, "7 Facts about Americans with Disabilities," Pew Research Center, July 27, 2017, http://www.pewresearch.org/fact-tank/2017/07/27/7-facts-about-americans-with-disabilities/; DisabledWorld: Towards Tomorrow, "Disability Statistics: Information, Charts, Graphs, Tables," updated September 28, 2018, https://www.disabled-world.com/disability/statistics/; and Lewis Kraus, *2016 Disability Statistics Annual Report* (Durham, NH: University of New Hampshire, 2017), https://disabilitycompendium.org/sites/default/files/user-uploads/2016_AnnualReport.pdf.
45. See Jeanine Braithwaite and Daniel Mont, "Disability and Poverty: A Survey of World Bank Poverty Assessments and Implications," *ALTER, European Journal of Disability Research* 3 (2009): 219–32. Regarding the challenges of measuring poverty levels among people with disability, see Nora Groce, Gayatri Kembhavi, Sheila Wirz, Raymond Lang, Jean-Francois Trani, and Maria Kett, "Poverty and Disability: A Critical Review of the Literature in Low and Middle-Income Countries," Working Paper Series 16 (2011), Leonard Cheshire Disability and Inclusive Development Centre, University College London, https://www.ucl.ac.uk/lc-ccr/centrepublications/workingpapers/WP16_Poverty_and_Disability_review.pdf.
46. Cf. Michael J. Klarman, *From Jim Crow to Civil Rights: The Supreme Court and the Struggle for Racial Equality* (New York: Oxford University Press, 2004).
47. United States Department of Education, Office of Civil Rights, Philadelphia Office, "Verbal and Psychological Abuse," 2019, https://disabilityjustice.org/verbal-and-psychological-abuse/.
48. See Lisa Jones, Mark A. Bellis, Sara Wood, Karen Hughes, Ellie McCoy, Lindsay Eckley, Geoff Bates, Christopher Mikton, Tom Shakespeare, and Alana Officer, "Prevalence and Risk of Violence against Children with Disabilities: A Systematic Review and Meta-Analysis of Observational Studies," *The Lancet* 380.9845 (2012): 899–907; and Karen Hughes, Mark A. Bellis, Lisa Jones, Sara Wood, Geoff Bates, Lindsay Eckley, Ellen McCoy, Christopher Mikton, Tom Shakespeare, and Alana Officer, "Prevalence and Risk of Violence against Adults with Disabilities: A Systematic Review and Meta-Analysis of Observational Studies," *The Lancet* 379.9826 (2012): 1621–29.
49. See US Department of Justice, Civil Rights Division, "Project Civic Access," ADA Information and Technical Assistance on the Americans with Disabilities Act, n.d., https://www.ada.gov/ta-pubs-pg2.htm.

50. See Iozzio, "Norms Matter."
51. Among others, see Colin Barnes and Geof Mercer, *Disability* (Cambridge, UK: Polity, 2003).

Chapter 3. Natural Law and the Common Good

1. See Thomas Aquinas, *Summa theologiae*, I.II. 94.2.c.
2. See Martha Nussbaum, "Nature, Function, and Capability: Aristotle on Political Distribution," in *Marx and Aristotle*, ed. George E. McCarthy, 44–70 (Savage, MD: Rowman & Littlefield, 2006); Suzanne DeCrane, *Aquinas, Feminism and the Common Good* (Washington, DC: Georgetown University Press, 2004), 34–39; and Paulus Bambang Irawan, "A Capability to Promote the Common Good," *Jurnal Teologi* 5.1 (2016): 1–14.
3. Among others, see Vatican II, *Dignitas humanae: Declaration on Religious Liberty* (1965); Vatican II, *Gaudium et spes: Constitution on the Church in the Modern World* (1965); Catholic Church, *The Catechism of the Catholic Church* (1993); and United States Conference of Catholic Bishops, "Life and Dignity of the Human Person," 2018, http://www.usccb.org/beliefs-and -teachings/what-we-believe/catholic-social-teaching/life-and-dignity-of -the-human-person.cfm.
4. Nussbaum articulates the capabilities as human rights to life; bodily health; bodily integrity; senses, imagination, and thought; emotions; practical reason; affiliation; concern for other species; play; and control over one's environment. See Martha Nussbaum, "Capabilities and Human Rights," *Fordham Law Review* 66.2 (1997): 273–300, esp. 287–88.
5. "All animals are equal, but some animals are more equal than others." George Orwell, *Animal Farm* (London, UK: Secker & Warburg, 1945), chap. 10.
6. John XXIII, *Mater et Magistra* (1961), #65, http://w2.vatican.va/content/john -xxiii/en/encyclicals/documents/hf_j-xxiii_enc_15051961_mater.html.
7. See Kirkbride Buildings, http://www.kirkbridebuildings.com; and Carla Joinson, "Asylums and Insanity Treatments 1800–1935," Indians, Insanity, and American History Blog, n.d., http://cantonasylumforinsaneindians.com /history_blog/.
8. Among others, see Victoria Brignell, "When the Disabled Were Segregated," *New Statesman America*, December 15, 2010, https://www.newstatesman .com/society/2010/12/disabled-children-british; Human Rights Watch, "They Stay until They Die," 2016, https://www.hrw.org/report/2018/05 /23/they-stay-until-they-die/lifetime-isolation-and-neglect-institutions

-people; and Molly McCully Brown, *The Virginia State Colony for Epileptics and Feebleminded* (New York: Persea Books, 2017).

9. See Mark 3:28–29.

10. Aquinas, *Summa theologiae*, I.II. 91.2.c, 91.3.c.

11. On the metaphysics of the human act, see Aquinas, *Summa theologiae*, I.II. 9-10. See also James F. Keenan, S.J., *Goodness and Rightness in Thomas Aquinas's* Summa Theologiae (Washington, DC: Georgetown University Press, 1992), 38–91; and Mary Jo Iozzio, *Self-Determination and the Moral Act: A Study of the Contributions of Odon Lottin, O.S.B.* (Leuven, Belgium: Peeters, 1995), 11–52.

12. Aquinas, *Summa theologiae*, I.II. 94.2c (my emphasis).

13. Aquinas, *Summa theologiae*, I.II. 94.4c.

14. Aquinas, *Summa theologiae*, II.II. 58.11c.

15. See Aquinas, *Commentary on Aristotle's* Nicomachean Ethics, trans. C. I. Litzinger (Notre Dame, IN: Dumb Ox Books, 1993), Book V, Lectures IV and V.

16. Aquinas, *Summa theologiae*, II.II. 58.2c.

17. Aquinas, *Summa theologiae*, II.II. 61.1c and 2c.

18. "Reasonable accommodation is any modification or adjustment to a job or the work environment that will enable a qualified applicant or employee with a disability to participate in the application process or to perform essential job functions. Reasonable accommodation also includes adjustments to assure that a qualified individual with a disability has rights and privileges in employment equal to those of employees without disabilities." ADA National Network, "The Americans with Disabilities Act: Questions and Answers," 2013, https://adata.org/publication/ADA-faq-booklet.

19. See Amartya Sen, *Inequality Reexamined* (Cambridge, MA: Harvard University Press, 1992); and Martha Nussbaum, *Women and Human Development: The Capabilities Approach* (Cambridge: Cambridge University Press, 2001).

20. John Locke, *Two Treatises of Government* (Cambridge: Cambridge University Press, 1988 [1694]).

21. Carlos A. Ball, "Autonomy, Justice, and Disability," *UCLA Law Review* 47 (1999–2000): 624.

22. See Robert P. O'Quinn, "The Americans with Disabilities Act: Time for Amendments," Policy Analysis No. 158 (August 9, 1991), Cato Institute, https://www.cato.org/publications/policy-analysis/americans-disabilities -act-time-amendmentsm; and David Boaz, "Libertarianism," Cato Institute, n.d., https://www.cato.org/research/libertarianism.

23. See Leslie Fiedler, *The Tyranny of the Normal* (Boston: David R. Godine, 1996).

24. Augustine of Hippo, as quoted in Sydney J. Harris, *Majority of One* (Boston: Houghton Mifflin, 1957).

Chapter 4. *Imago Dei*, Theological Anthropology, and Catholic Social Teaching

1. Karl Rahner, SJ, is arguably the first of twentieth-century Catholic scholars claiming that all theology must be of necessity theological anthropology. See Karl Rahner, "Theology and Anthropology," in *Theological Investigations IX*, trans. G. Harrison, 28–45 (London: Darton, Longman & Todd, 1972).

2. See Isaiah 52:14, 53:3, 7, 8.

3. To the extent that the nondisabled are threatened by those among them who have putatively greater strength, height, beauty, intelligence, resources, and the like, they may experience internalized oppression and could experience overt forms of discrimination, bullying, and other violence against them. See Mark B. Tappan, "Reframing Internalized Oppression and Internalized Domination: From the Psychological to the Sociocultural," *Teachers College Record* 108.19 (2006): 2115–44.

4. See Nancy L. Eiesland, *The Disabled God: Toward a Liberatory Theology of Disability* (Nashville, TN: Abingdon, 1994).

5. Of course, people with disability already embody the ideal that is diversity; affirmation is the social deconstruction of hegemonic denials of their inclusion as well as the paradigmatic expression of the norm.

6. See Catherine Mowry LaCugna, *God for Us: The Trinity and Christian Life* (New York: HarperCollins, 1991).

7. See Gloria L. Schaab, *The Creative Suffering of the Triune God: An Evolutionary Theology* (New York: Oxford University Press, 2007); Mary Jo Iozzio, "Genetic Anomaly or Genetic Diversity: Thinking in the Key of Disability," *Theological Studies* 66.3 (2005): 862–81; Mary Jo Iozzio, "Thinking about Disabilities with Justice, Liberation, and Mercy," *Horizons* 36.1 (2009): 32–49; and Mary Jo Iozzio, "Radical Dependence and the *Imago Dei*: Bioethical Implication of Access to Healthcare for People with Disabilities," *Christian Bioethics* 23.2 (2017): 234–60.

8. See Thomas Aquinas, *Summa theologiae*, I. 27–32; and Herbert McCabe, OP, "Aquinas on the Trinity," *New Blackfriars* 80 (1999): 268–90.

9. Eiesland, *The Disabled God*, 11.

10. Eiesland, 14.

11. See Iozzio, "Norms Matter: A Hermeneutic of Disability/a Theological Anthropology of Radical Dependence," *ET-Studies* 4.1 (2013): 89–106.

12. See Deborah Creamer, "Theological Accessibility: The Contribution of Disability," *Disability Studies Quarterly* 26.4 (2006), http://dsq-sds.org/article/view/812/987; and Scot Danforth, "Liberation Theology of Disability and the Option for the Poor," *Disability Studies Quarterly* 25.3 (2005), http://dsq-sds.org/article/view/572/749.

13. On the larger implications of the Genesis text in regard to both the plural Elohim and the creation of the first human beings, see Ronald Hendel, Chana Kronfeld, and Ilana Pardes, "Gender and Sexuality," in *Reading Genesis: Ten Methods*, ed. Ronald Hendel, 71–91 (New York: Cambridge University Press, 2010).

14. See World Council of Churches, "Mission from the Margins: What We Do," 2019, https://www.oikoumene.org/en/what-we-do/just-and-inclusive-communities.

15. See Central Committee, "New Affirmation on Mission and Evangelization," in *Together towards Life: Mission and Evangelism in Changing Landscapes* (Geneva: World Council of Churches, 2013), #5–6, https://www.oikoumene.org/en/resources/publications/TogethertowardsLife_MissionandEvangelism.pdf.

16. See Council for World Mission, *Unmasking Empire* (Singapore, SI: CWM Ltd., 2018), https://issuu.com/cwmission/docs/cwm_-_unmasking_empire; Council for World Mission, *Mission in the Context of Empire: Theology Statement 2010* (Singapore: CWM Ltd., 2010); and Walter Wink, *The Powers That Be: Theology for a New Millennium* (New York: Doubleday/Random House, 1998).

17. Pontifical Council for Justice and Peace, *Compendium of the Social Doctrine of the Church* (Vatican City: Libreria Editrice Vaticana, 2004), §§144, 145, 148.

18. On lament and its necessary connection to past injustice, see especially Emilie M. Townes, *Breaking the Fine Rain of Death: African America Health Issues and a Womanist Ethics of Care* (Eugene, OR: Wipf & Stock, 1998), 9–25.

19. See Johann Baptist Metz, *Faith in History and Society: Toward a Fundamental Practical Theology* (New York: Seabury, 1980).

20. Paul VI, "If You Want Peace, Work for Justice," Message for the World Day of Peace, January 1, 1972, http://w2.vatican.va/content/paul-vi/en/messages/peace/documents/hf_p-vi_mes_19711208_v-world-day-for-peace.html.

21. Pontifical Council for Justice and Peace, *Compendium*, §494.

22. Caritas Internationalis, "Mission," n.d., https://www.caritas.org/who-we -are/mission/. See also "Vision," n.d., https://www.caritas.org/who-we-are /vision/; and "Our Work," n.d., https://www.caritas.org/what-we-do/.

23. Caritas Australia, Global Issues, "Disability," 2019, https://www.caritas.org .au/learn/global-poverty-issues/disability.

24. See Francis, *Laudato Si': Encyclical Letter On Care for Our Common Home* (Vatican City: Libreria Editrice Vaticana, 2015), http://w2.vatican.va /content/francesco/en/encyclicals/documents/papa-francesco_20150524 _enciclica-laudato-si.html.

25. See Suzanne E. Evans, *Forgotten Crimes: The Holocaust and People with Disabilities* (Chicago: Ivan R. Dee, 2004); Michael Burleigh, *Death and Deliverance: Euthanasia in Germany c. 1900–1945* (Cambridge: Cambridge University Press, 1994); Thomas L. McDonald, "John XXIII and the Jews," The Catholic World Report, April 3, 2014, https://www.catholic worldreport.com/2014/04/03/john-xxiii-and-the-jews/; and United States Holocaust Memorial Museum, "Nazi Persecution of the Disabled: Murder of the 'Unfit,'" n.d., https://www.ushmm.org/information/exhibitions /online-exhibitions/special-focus/nazi-persecution-of-the-disabled.

26. See John XXIII, *Pacem in Terris* (1963), §11, http://w2.vatican.va/content /john-xxiii/en/encyclicals/documents/hf_j-xxiii_enc_11041963_pacem .html.

27. John Paul II references people with disability once in *Evangelium Vitae* (1995), §63, http://w2.vatican.va/content/john-paul-ii/en/encyclicals /documents/hf_jp-ii_enc_25031995_evangelium-vitae.html. Francis references people with disability once in *Laudato Si'*, §117, and four times in the postsynodal apostolic exhortation *Amoris Laetitia* (2015), §§47, 82, 197, http://w2.vatican.va/content/dam/francesco/pdf/apost_exhortations /documents/papa-francesco_esortazione-ap_20160319_amoris-laetitia _en.pdf.

28. See "Press Release: Jubilee for Those Who Are Ill and Disabled," Jubilee of Mercy, 2016, http://www.im.va/content/gdm/en/news/evidenza/2016 -06-09-pcpne.html. See also Carol Glatz, "Church Can't Be Blind, Deaf, to People with Special Needs, Pope Says," Catholic News Service, October 23, 2017, https://www.catholicnews.com/services/englishnews/2017 /church-cant-be-blind-deaf-to-people-with-special-needs-pope-says .cfm; and Ines San Martin, "Pope Decries 'Eugenic Tendency' to Eradicate People with Disabilities," Crux: Taking the Catholic Pulse, October 21, 2017, https://cruxnow.com/vatican/2017/10/21/pope-decries-eugenic -tendency-eradicate-people-disabilities/.

29. Committee for the Jubilee Day of the Community with Persons with Disabilities, "Preparation for the Jubilee Day 3 December 2000, Part One," 2000, http://www.vatican.va/jubilee_2000/jubilevents/jub_disabled_2000 1203_scheda1_en.htm.

30. Committee for the Jubilee Day of the Community with Persons with Disabilities, "Preparation for the Jubilee Day 3 December 2000, Part Two," 2000, http://www.vatican.va/jubilee_2000/jubilevents/jub_disabled_2000 1203_scheda2_en.htm.

31. Committee for the Jubilee Day of the Community with Persons with Disabilities, "Preparation for the Jubilee Day 3 December 2000, Part Three," 2000, http://www.vatican.va/jubilee_2000/jubilevents/jub_disabled_2000 1203_scheda3_en.htm.

32. Committee for the Jubilee Day of the Community with Persons with Disabilities, "Preparation for the Jubilee Day 3 December 2000, Part Four," 2000, http://www.vatican.va/jubilee_2000/jubilevents/jub_disabled_2000 1203_scheda4_en.htm.

33. Committee for the Jubilee Day of the Community with Persons with Disabilities, "Preparation for the Jubilee Day 3 December 2000, Part Five," 2000, https://www.vatican.va/jubilee_2000/jubilevents/jub_disabled_20001203 _scheda5_en.htm.

34. See Michelle R. Nario-Redmond, *Ableism: The Causes and Consequences of Disability Prejudice* (Hoboken, NJ: Wiley, 2020), 166–219.

35. Eiesland, *The Disabled God*, 75.

36. "Pope Meets with Participants in Vatican Disability Conference," October 21, 2017, Vatican News, https://www.vaticannews.va/en/pope/news /2017-10/time-for-persons-with-disabilities-to-become-catechists.html.

37. Eiesland, *The Disabled God*, 83.

38. USCCB, "Pastoral Statement on People with Disabilities," 1978), #1, available at National Catholic Partnership on Disability, http://www.ncpd.org /views-news-policy/policy/church/bishops/pastoral. As many recognize today, some of these terms have been replaced, rightly, by the terms "cognitive disabilities," "developmental disabilities," "learning disabilities," and "physical impairments."

39. USCCB, "Guidelines for the Celebration of the Sacraments with Persons with Disabilities," 1995 (revised 2017), http://www.usccb.org/about/divine -worship/policies/guidelines-sacraments-persons-with-disabilities.cfm.

40. USCCB, "Guidelines," #2.

41. Pontifical Council for Justice and Peace, *Compendium*, §192.

42. See "Universal Design," The Center for An Accessible Society, n.d., http:// www.accessiblesociety.org/topics/universaldesign/; and "About Universal

Design for Learning," CAST: Until Learning Has No Limits, 2019, http://
www.cast.org/our-work/about-udl.html#.XIMOuRNKiCd.

43. "Creating a Universally Designed Ministry," National Catholic Partnership
on Disability, 2014, http://www.ncpd.org/accessible-design.

44. See National Catholic Partnership on Disability, *Opening Doors to Welcome
and Justice to Parishioners with Disabilities* (Washington, DC: National
Catholic Office for Persons with Disabilities, 2003), 8–11.

45. See Vatican II, *Lumen gentium: Dogmatic Constitution on the Church*, §11
(1964).

Chapter 5. A Preferential Justice for Those Who
Are Poor or Otherwise Marginalized

1. See Norbert F. Lohfink, S.J., *Option for the Poor: The Basic Principle of Liberation Theology in Light of the Bible* (Berkeley, CA: Bibal Press, 1987); and
Scott Danforth, "Liberation Theology of Disability and the Option for the
Poor," *Disability Studies Quarterly* 25.3 (2005), http://dsq-sds.org/article
/view/572/749.

2. Among others, see Gustavo Gutierrez, *A Theology of Liberation: History,
Politics, and Salvation* (Maryknoll, NY: Orbis Books, 1973, revised ed.
1988); Leonardo Boff and Clodovis Boff, *Introducing Liberation Theology*
(Maryknoll, NY: Orbis Books, 1986); and Jon Sobrino, *Spirituality of Liberation: Toward Political Holiness* (Maryknoll, NY: Orbis Books, 1988).

3. For example, from ancient times to the present, women who have been
racialized and those who are lesbian, gay, bisexual, transgender, queer,
and intersexed have been (recent) recipients of opportunities to advance
in their status with recognition and disavowal of the social constructions
of their "otherness" as well as with access to education, employment, and
other common goods.

4. See United Nations Global Compact, *Poverty Footprint: A People-
Centered Approach to Assessing Business Impacts on Sustainable Development* (2015), https://www.unglobalcompact.org/docs/issues_doc/human
_rights/PovertyFootprint.pdf.

5. Cases of noncompliance are often settled without legal recourse; nevertheless, the US Department of Justice, Civil Rights Division, publishes court
cases and their outcomes to date. See ADA.gov, "ADA Enforcement," n.d.,
https://www.ada.gov/enforce_current.htm.

6. Mary Jo Iozzio, "Solidarity: Restoring Communion with Those Who Are
Disabled," *Journal of Religion, Disability & Health* 15.2 (2011): 140.

7. See John 13:31–35. Consider also Irenaeus's theo-anthropological insight about humankind: the glory of God is (the human being) fully alive. Irenaeus, *Against Heresies*, in *Ante-Nicene Fathers*, Vol. 1, ed. Philip Schaff (Grand Rapids, MI: Wm. B. Eerdmans, reprint 2001 of New York: Christian Literature Publishing, 1885), Book 4, chap. XX: 7.

8. In what was to be a prepared address to participants at a meeting promoted by the Italian Episcopal Conference in advance of the Extraordinary Jubilee of Mercy for the Sick and Persons with Disabilities (June 12, 2016), Pope Francis went off script to respond to questions from the audience. To one of the little girls who asked what advice would the Pope give to a priest who doesn't accept everyone, he answered, "Close the doors of the church, please! Either everyone or no one." Pope Francis, "Address to Participants in the Convention for Persons with Disabilities Promoted," Vatican City, Paul VI Audience Hall, June 11, 2016, https://w2.vatican.va /content/francesco/en/speeches/2016/june/documents/papa-francesco _20160611_convegno-disabili.html.

9. In addition to the initiatives of the National Catholic Partnership on Disability and the Committee for the Jubilee Day of the Community with Persons with Disabilities, "The Person with Disabilities: The Duties of the Civil and Ecclesial Community," July 17, 2000, http://www.vatican.va /jubilee_2000/jubilevents/jub_disabled_20001203_scheda5_en.htm, see the Pontifical Council for Promoting the New Evangelization, "Catechesis and Persons with Disabilities," II International Congress on Catechesis, Pontifical Urbaniana University, Rome, October 20–22, 2017, http://www .pcpne.va/content/pcpne/en/attivita/catechesi/convegno-internazionale -di-catechesi.html; and World Council of Churches Central Committee, "A Church of All for All," Document No. PLEN 1.1 (Geneva: World Council of Churches, 2003), #s 66–72, http://www.oikoumene.org/en/resources /documents/central-committee/2003/a-church-of-all-and-for-all.

10. World Council of Churches, "A Church of All for All," #68.

11. On moral luck, among others, see Lisa Tessman, *Burdened Virtues: Virtue Ethics for Liberatory Struggles* (New York: Oxford University Press, 2005); and Joseph J. Kotva Jr., *The Christian Case for Virtue Ethics* (Washington, DC: Georgetown University Press, 1996).

12. See WHO, *International Classification of Functioning, Disability, and Health* (Geneva: World Health Organization, 2001), 4.

13. In addition to the sources cited in chapter 2, note 48, see WHO, "Violence against Adults and Children with Disabilities," n.d., https://www.who.int /disabilities/violence/en/; and The National Coalition Against Domestic

Violence, "Domestic Violence and People with Disabilities: What to Know, Why It Matters, and How to Help" (March 13, 2018), https://ncadv.org /blog/posts/domestic-violence-and-people-with-disabilities; and National Domestic Violence Hotline, "Abuse in Disability Communities," n.d., https://www.thehotline.org/resources/abuse-in-disability-communities/.

14. Among others, see Debbie Lillo, *Doing Life Together: Building a Community for Families Affected by Disability* (Agoura Hills, CA: Joni and Friends International Disability Center, 2017); and Mike Dobes, *Go Make Disciples: Embracing People Affected by Disability through Mentoring Relationships* (Agoura Hills, CA: Joni and Friends International Disability Center, 2018).

15. See Mark T. Finney, "*Servile Supplicium*: Shame and the Deuteronomic Curse—Crucifixion in Its Cultural Context," *Journal of Bible and Culture* 43.3 (2013): 124–34.

16. See John Swinton, *Becoming Friends of Time: Disability, Timefullness, and Gentle Discipleship* (Waco, TX: Baylor University Press, 2016); and Jason Reimer Grieg, *Reconsidering Intellectual Disability: L'Arche, Medical Ethics, and Christian Friendship* (Washington, DC: Georgetown University Press, 2015).

17. Hak Joon Lee, "Kingdom and *Kenosis*: The Mind of Christ in Paul's Ethics," *Theology, News and Notes* 60.2 (2013): 12.

18. Here and elsewhere I include by way of addition pronouns inclusive of gender nonbinary terms so as to avoid the "implied gender," which for most of the documents of the Church assumes that references to he, him, or man/men imply generically women too. More recently, the gender binary has been challenged, resulting in the addition of ze/zir/zirs to avoid potentially harmful assumptions about another person or a conflation of all genders under the umbrella man/men. See "Pronouns Matter," n.d., https://www.mypronouns.org/.

19. Committee for the Jubilee Day of the Community with Persons with Disabilities, "Preparation for the Jubilee Day 3 December 2000," July 17, 2000, http://www.vatican.va/jubilee_2000/jubilevents/jub_disabled_20001203 _scheda5_en.htm. While to valorise points to the positive value inherent in a person or a thing, in this context it may lead to condescension of the kind to which many persons with disability have experienced. As Andrew Purlang notes, "it feels like empty emoting that has more to do with a nondisabled person's own personality and emotional investments than the disabled person's actual character or achievements." Andrew Purlang, "3 Disability Microaggressions and Why They Matter," *Forbes*, February 26,

2022, https://www.forbes.com/sites/andrewpulrang/2022/02/26/5-disability
-microaggressions-and-why-they-matter/?sh=2f34182d7e17. Alternately,
recognition includes acknowledgment of everyone's gifts and leads to rec-
onciliation and solidarity.

20. Archbishop Rino Fisichella, president, Pontifical Council for Promoting
the New Evangelization, "The Profession of Faith: 'To Believe'—One's
Response to God Who Reveals Himself," Introductory Remarks, Vatican City, Paul VI Hall, October 20, 2017, http://www.pcpne.va/content
/pcpne/en/news/2017-10-20-agensir2.html.

21. Pope Francis, "Address to Participants in the Conference Organized by the
Pontifical Council for Promoting New Evangelization," Vatican City, Clem-
entine Hall, October 21, 2017, http://w2.vatican.va/content/francesco
/en/speeches/2017/october/documents/papa-francesco_20171021
_convegno-pcpne.html. I have replaced the term "handicap," defined as a
disadvantage and that has a history of stigma against persons who differ
from the putative normal, with "disability," the preferred term of activists
and used in the Americans with Disabilities Act as well as in the UN and
WHO initiatives.

22. Among others, see Joseph Luders, "The Economics of Movement Success: Business Response to Civil Rights Mobilization," *American Journal of
Sociology* 111.4 (2006): 963–98; Tania Sourdin and Naomi Burstyner, "Justice Delayed Is Justice Denied," *Victoria University Law and Justice Journal*
4.1 (2014): 46–60.

23. See Jonathan Holland, Patrick Gilger, S.J., and Thomas P. Gaunt, S.J., "Disabilities in Parishes across the United States: How Parishes in the United
States Accommodate and Serve People with Disabilities," Center for Applied
Research in the Apostolate, Georgetown University, Summer 2016, https://
cara.georgetown.edu/Disabilities.pdf.

24. On the delays of compliance with the Americans with Disabilities Act
see, among many others, Sean Pevsner, "ADA Reform: Justice Delayed Is
Justice Denied," Brewminate, July 21, 2017, https://brewminate.com/ada
-reform-justice-delayed-is-justice-denied/; Matan Koch, "Don't Let Rights
Delayed Become Rights Denied under the ADA," ACLU/American Civil
Liberties Union, October 26, 2017, https://www.aclu.org/blog/dont-let
-rights-delayed-become-rights-denied-under-ada; and Center for Disability Rights, "Access Delayed Is Justice Denied," 2012, http://cdrnys.org/blog
/advocacy/access-delayed-is-justice-denied-again/.

25. See Michael Ashley Stein, "Disability Human Rights," *California Law Review*
95.1 (2007): 75–121.

26. See Pauline Otieno, "Biblical and Theological Perspectives on Disability: Implications on the Rights of Persons with Disability in Kenya," *Disability Studies Quarterly* 29.4 (2009), http://dsq-sds.org/article/view/988/1164.

27. Cf. Matt 25:31–46.

28. I take the notion of "function" in the sense of an underlying operation or role to which a "symbol," "person," "action," "object," "maxim," etc. refers abstractly or concretely, that is, what is proper to "it" that distinguishes "it" from other kinds of things. Among others, see Elizabeth A. Johnson, *She Who Is: The Mystery of God in Feminist Theological Discourse* (New York: Crossroad, 1996); Paul Ricoeur, *The Symbolism of Evil*, trans. Emerson Buchanan (New York: Harper & Row, 1967); and Gloria L. Schaab, "Sacred Symbol as Theological Text," *Heythrop Journal* 50.1 (2009): 58–73.

29. Pontifical Council for Justice and Peace, *Compendium of the Social Doctrine of the Church*, §§172, 175, 182.

30. See Wouter Peters, Jo Dirix, and Sigrid Sterckx, "Towards an Integration of the Ecological Space Paradigm and the Capabilities Approach," *Journal of Agricultural and Environmental Ethics* 28 (2015): 479–96. On subsistence as a threshold, see Nussbaum, *Frontiers of Justice*, especially chaps. 4 and 5.

31. Christopher J. H. Wright, *Old Testament Ethics for the People of God* (Downers Grove, IL: InterVarsity, 2004), 256, 257, 259.

32. See Kanti Lal Das, "Preferential Treatment: A Means of Social Justice," *Journal of East-West Thought* 7.2 (2017): 49–63.

33. See Thomas Aquinas, *Summa theologiae*, I.II.61.1c and 2c; and Aristotle, *Nicomachean Ethics*, Book V.3.

34. See John L. McKenzie, "The Gospel According to Matthew" (#74), and Caroll Stuhlmueller, C.P., "The Gospel According to Luke" (#75), in *The Jerome Biblical Commentary*, ed. Raymond E. Brown, S.S., Joseph A. Fitzmyer, S.J., and Roland E. Murphy, O.Carm. (Englewood Cliffs, NJ: Prentice Hall, 1968); and Daniel J. Harrington, S.J., "The Gospel According to Matthew" (#41), and Robert J, Karras, "The Gospel According to Luke" (#42), in *The New Jerome Biblical Commentary*, ed. Raymond E. Brown, S.S., Joseph A. Fitzmyer, S.J., and Roland E. Murphy, O.Carm. (Englewood Cliffs, NJ: Prentice Hall, 1990).

35. See Aquinas, *Summa theologiae*, "Of the Good and Evil in Human Acts" and "Of the Goodness and Malice of the Interior Act of the Will," I.II.18 and 19; and James F. Keenan, S.J., *Goodness and Rightness in Thomas Aquinas's* Summa Theologiae (Washington, DC: Georgetown University Press, 1992), 65–91.

36. See Elizabeth A. Johnson, *Friends of God and Prophets: A Feminist Theological Reading of the Communion of Saints* (New York: Continuum, 1999).

Conclusion: Inclusion in Place of Neglect

1. I take a certain liberty with this claim; the metaphorical analogy is inclusive. Nevertheless, as I consider the *imago Dei* conferred on all human beings, I consider that any insult to the *imago Dei* is a sin committed against God. I suspect that obstinacy may be the species of blasphemy I here entertain as resistance to the truth about human beings, from the least to the greatest. Cf. Thomas Aquinas, *Summa theologiae*, II.II.14.3; John Paul II, *Apostolic Exhortation Reconciliatio et Paenitentia* (December 2, 1984), §18; and the *Catechism of the Catholic Church* (Vatican City: Libreria Editrice Vaticana, 1993) #1864.

2. See Daniel J. Harrington, S.J., and James F. Keenan, S.J., "Politics from a Marginal Perspective," *Jesus and Virtue Ethics: Building Bridges between New Testament Studies and Virtue Ethics* (Lanham, MD: Sheed & Ward, 2002), 105–19.

3. See Paulo Freire, *Pedagogy of the Oppressed* (New York: Bloomsbury Academic, 1993).

4. In addition to Mark T. Finney, "*Servile Supplicium*: Shame and the Deuteronomic Curse—Crucifixion in Its Cultural Context," *Journal of Bible and Culture* 43.3 (2013): 124–34, see David Tombs, "Crucifixion, State Terror, and Sexual Abuse," *Union Seminary Quarterly Review* 53.1–2 (1999): 89–109; and François Pieter Retief and Louise Cilliers, "The History and Pathology of Crucifixion," *South Africa Medical Journal* 93.12 (2003): 938–41.

5. Mary Jo Iozzio, "God Bends Over Backwards to Accommodate Humankind . . . While the Civil Rights Acts and the Americans with Disabilities Act Require [Only] the Minimum," *Journal of Moral Theology* 6.SI 2 (2017): 28–29.

6. Council for World Mission, *Mission in the Context of Empire: Theology Statement 2010* (Singapore: CWM Ltd., 2010), 4–5.

— INDEX —

disability: cognitive, 7, 10, 21, 26, 37, 53;
developmental, 7, 10, 18, 20, 37, 42;
intellectual, 7, 34, 45, 51, 61; physical,
7, 8, 9, 10, 20, 26, 42, 45, 53, 61, 75;
sensory, 8, 10, 19, 26
disability studies, 1, 4, 35, 51
disabled God, 51, 53–54, 68, 69, 71, 87
disciple/discipleship, 64, 66, 73, 77, 80,
84, 87, 89
discrimination, 6, 8, 15, 18, 20–21, 24,
26, 29, 37–38, 45, 48, 57, 63
diversity, 9–10, 16–17, 18, 22, 33–34, 43,
50, 51, 52–54, 67–70, 85–86
dualism(s), 17, 53

economic/socioeconomic, 9, 10, 25, 34,
35, 36, 45, 78
Eiesland, Nancy, 51, 53, 60, 61
empire, 57–58, 88, 89
employment, 6, 9–10, 25, 27, 29, 30, 32,
35, 36, 72, 79, 87
energy, 29, 40
equality, 25, 28, 29, 45, 46, 56, 62
eugenics, 15, 16
exclusion, 11, 21, 22, 37, 63, 68, 86, 88
experimentation, 16, 72
exploitation, 15, 16, 24, 62, 66

Farahanchi, Nina, 5–6, 11
fecund, 17, 73, 86
fecund imaginary, 58, 68–69
feminist, 51, 86
Fisichella, Archbishop Rino, 74
Foucault, Michel, 20, 53
Francis (pope), 59–61, 74
freedom(s), 31, 34, 35, 44, 47
friendship, 35, 42, 58, 63, 65–70, 73,
80–81
functioning capabilities, 33–35, 40–41,
44–45, 47, 84
fundamental freedoms, 26, 27, 31

Gaudet, Matthew, 3, 40, 124
gay, 38, 43

gender, 9, 28, 29, 33, 35, 43, 47, 51,
64–65, 67, 85
genetics, 4, 16, 19
Good News, 55, 57, 69–70, 80, 84, 87, 89
grace(s), 53, 63

Handicap International, 31
hegemony/hegemonic, 1, 11, 18–21, 36,
43, 47, 55, 70, 86, 89
hermeneutic, 18, 33, 62, 66, 88
heterosexism, 21
heterosexual, 17, 19, 53
hierarchy/hierarchies, 17, 74, 85
HIV/AIDS, 27, 28
Holy Spirit, 53, 69, 84
housing, 6, 25, 32, 36, 48
human dignity, 11, 37, 54, 55–56, 64, 66
human flourishing, 1, 6, 18, 36, 40–41,
45–46, 66
human rights, 6, 26, 33, 57–58
hunger, 28, 29, 82

imaginary, 58, 68, 85
imagination, 23, 49
imagine, 34, 35, 47
imago Dei, 3, 42, 50–56, 69, 84–85
impairment, 7–9, 63, 64
Incarnate Word of God, 50–51, 53, 69
inclusion/inclusive, 7, 12, 17, 29, 31,
60–61, 63–64, 74, 76, 80–81
independence, 18, 19
Indigenous, 38, 86
infrastructure, 29, 30, 48, 71
institution/institutionalization, 9, 15–16,
25, 29, 42, 72
interdependence, 26, 39, 62
intersex, 38, 43
Islam, 2

Jesus, 15, 50, 51, 54, 64, 69–71, 77, 80, 87
Jewish Federation of North America, 2
Job, book of, 14
John XXIII (pope): *Mater et Magistra*,
42; *Pacem in Terris*, 59

— ABOUT THE AUTHOR —

MARY JO IOZZIO, PhD, STL, is a professor of moral theology at Boston College School of Theology and Ministry and teaches social ethics, fundamental moral theology, and the critiques of systemic injustice with a special interest in disability studies, antiracism, feminist theology, gender, and access to the means of human flourishing. Before Boston College, Iozzio taught from 1993 to 2013 at Barry University, Miami Shores, Florida. She lectures and writes extensively on disability at the intersections of theological ethics, anthropology, and faith. She is an active member of the American Academy of Religion, Catholic Theological Ethics in the World Church, the Catholic Theological Society of America, and the Society of Christian Ethics. Iozzio served as Distinguished Professor and Austin & Ann O'Malley Chair in Bioethics at Loyola Marymount University (2019) and has been a recipient of the St. Elizabeth Ann Seton Award (2018), an awardee for research from Fondazione Bruno Kessler, Trento (2009), an Ambassador Jean Wilkowski International Fellow (2001–2), and a US Fulbright Senior Scholar (1998–99).

Iozzio is the author of *Self-Determination and the Moral Act: A Study of the Contributions of Odon Lottin, OSB* (Peeters, 1995) and *Radical Dependence: A Theo-Anthropological Ethic in the Key of Disability* (forthcoming); the series editor for *Content and Context in Theological Ethics* (Palgrave Macmillan); coeditor with Patricia Beattie Jung of *Sex & Gender: Christian Ethical Reflections* (Georgetown University Press, 2016); the principal editor of *Calling for Justice throughout the World: Catholic Women Theologians on the HIV/AIDS Pandemic* (Continuum,

2019); a past coeditor of the *Journal of the Society of Christian Ethics* (2006–13); a past facilitator of and contributor to the North American Forum for *The FIRST* newsletter of the Catholic Theological Ethicists in the World Church; a guest editor of and contributor to the *Journal of Moral Theology;* and a guest editor of and contributor to the *Journal of Religion, Disability & Health.* She has served as an Ethics Committee member for the New Jersey Home Health Assembly, Mercy Hospital–Miami, the Catholic Hospice of Miami–Dade County, the Coral Springs Medical Center, the Catholic Health Association, and the Bon Secours Health System and as a public member of the American Board of Plastic Surgery. Iozzio is a past member of the Board of the Society of Christian Ethics and the Board of the Catholic Theological Society of America. She was appointed to the American Academy of Religion Task Force on Disability (2001–6), followed by appointment as an inaugural member of its Standing Committee of the Status of People with Disabilities in the Profession (2013–16), and was a Steering Committee member and cochair of the Religion and Disability Studies Group (2013–19).

— ABOUT THE NARRATIVE — CONTRIBUTORS

JANA BENNETT, Mdiv, PhD, is a professor and chair of the Department of Religious Studies at the University of Dayton in Ohio. Her research interests include Christian ethics and Catholic moral theology on health, gender, feminist ethics, and marriage and singleness. Bennett is a frequent contributor to the Catholic Moral Theology discussion platform (https://catholicmoraltheology.com/) and is a catechist at Immaculate Conception Church in Dayton, her home parish.

MARIA CATALDO-CUNNIFF, MA, MTS, is a board-certified chaplain, formerly serving at Boston's Children's Hospital and Phillips Academy, Andover, Massachusetts. She is a member of the National Association of Catholic Chaplains. Cataldo-Cunniff makes meaning out of her own experience of disability, suffering, and hope with a view to empowering others with similar experiences to love themselves.

LORRAINE CUDDEBACK-GEDEON, MDiv, PhD, is the director of mission and ministry at Mercy High School, Baltimore, Maryland. She is a social justice educator involved in community-based service learning with practical expertise in disability studies, universal design, and Catholic social teaching. Cuddeback-Gedeon is a regular contributor to Catholic Moral Theology (https://catholicmoraltheology.com/) and Daily Theology (https://dailytheology.org/).

MATTHEW GAUDET, PhD, is a lecturer of engineering ethics at Santa Clara University, Santa Clara, California. His research lies at the intersections of moral theology and social science with a focus on disability ethics, ethics and technology, the ethics of war and peace, and university ethics. Gaudet is a frequent contributor and often editor of themed issues of the *Journal of Moral Theology*; he has contributed also to the *Encyclopedia of Disability History*, *America Magazine*, and the *National Catholic Reporter*.

MIGUEL J. ROMERO, MDiv, ThM, ThD, is an assistant professor of theological studies at Salve Regina University, Newport, Rhode Island. His research interests engage moral theology, Catholic social teaching, and the theological and philosophical considerations of disability and mental illness particularly through the lens of Thomas Aquinas's work.

SHAWNEE M. DANIELS-SYKES, RN, PhD, is a professor of ethics at Mount Mary University in Milwaukee, Wisconsin. Her research interests engage critical life issues at the intersections of race, class, and gender. Daniels-Sykes also teaches at the Institute for Black Catholic Studies at Xavier University of Louisiana and the Theology Collaborative for Ascension Health Care Executive Leadership, where she focuses on moral theology and Catholic social teaching.

VALERIE TURNER, MPhil, DMin, is retired from Barry University, Miami Shores, Florida. She was among the first web editors at Barry and fully engaged with communicating the institutional mission through electronic media. Turner's studies in ethics, bioethics, and patient spiritual care have focused on comforting patients in critical care and those in long-term rehabilitation centers.